WHAT IS SCIENCE EDUCATION FOR?

Institute of Ideas

WHAT IS SCIENCE EDUCATION FOR?

By **David Perks** with

Sir Richard Sykes

Professor Michael Reiss

Simon Singh

Baroness Mary Warnock

Andrew Hunt

Dr Eliot Forster

Dr Brian Iddon MP

Harriet Teare

Dr Gerry Lawless

Craig Fairnington

Jonathan Kestenbaum

Dr Michael Sargent

Steve Hearn

Ian Mellor

Helen O'Brien

Dr Peter Martin

Edited by **Tony Gilland**

This edition first published 2006 by Academy of Ideas Ltd.

Signet House

49-51 Farringdon Road

London EC1M 3JP

020 7269 9220

ISBN 1 904025 05 6

British Library Cataloguing in Publication Data

A catalogue record for this book is available from the British Library

Designed by Joe Ewart for Society

Printed by BAS

CONTENTS:

5 **FOREWORD**
Dr Eliot Forster

7 **INTRODUCTION**
Tony Gilland

9 **WHAT IS SCIENCE EDUCATION FOR?**
David Perks

RESPONSES:

35 **INSPIRATION THROUGH EXPERTISE**
Sir Richard Sykes

41 **LISTENING TO PUPILS**
Professor Michael Reiss

47 **CUT THE CRAP**
Simon Singh

53 **THE PATRONISING INDIGNITY OF TWENTY FIRST CENTURY SCIENCE**
Baroness Mary Warnock

57 **TWENTY FIRST CENTURY SCIENCE: THE CASE FOR CHANGE**
Andrew Hunt

63 **FOR SCIENTIFIC LITERACY AND PRACTICAL SCIENCE**
Dr Eliot Forster

67 **MAKING SCIENCE COOL**
Dr Brian Iddon MP

73 **EDUCATION SHOULDN'T BE FUN**
Harriet Teare

77 **A VICIOUS CIRCLE**
Dr Gerry Lawless

81 **WHAT INSPIRED ME**
Craig Fairnington

85 **NOTHING BUT FACTS?**
Jonathan Kestenbaum

89 **AN ELITIST POSITION**
Ian Mellor

93 **WORK WITH THE INDEPENDENT SECTOR**
Steve Hearn

97 **WHAT A RESEARCH INSTITUTE CAN CONTRIBUTE**
Dr Michael Sargent

101 **WAIT FOR THE EVIDENCE**
Helen O'Brien

105 **A LACK OF SELF-BELIEF**
Dr Peter Martin

109 **REPLY**
David Perks

115 **BIOGRAPHIES**

FOREWORD

Dr Eliot Forster

Vice President of Development, EU and Asia, Pfizer Global Research & Development

Every August, prompted by GCSE and A-level results, the UK has its annual debate about the state of education. Two recurring themes dominate the news media: 'Are kids really getting brighter or are standards dropping?' and 'What can be done to halt the rapid decline in the number of children studying traditional science subjects?'

Of the two issues, it is the latter which should concern us more. The evidence is indisputable – there are fewer and fewer students studying science beyond GCSE level. If left unchecked, this is a trend that will have negative and far-reaching consequences for us all.

At Pfizer, innovative science is at the core of what we do – without it, we would simply be unable to discover, develop and manufacture new medicines. When our researchers have a new idea about how a disease might be treated more effectively, they are taking the first step on a long, complex and often convoluted journey to a new medicine. Once they have found a lead compound, they have to re-design, test, modify and re-test it countless times before they reach a point where they have sufficient confidence to begin clinical trials on people. And even then, after years of work by medicinal chemists and biologists, the majority of compounds do not meet the safety and efficacy demands we make of them and so do not reach patients.

If there is one factor that determines our ability to succeed more than any other, it is the quality of our scientists. But it is not just Pfizer's future that depends on the ability of the education system to produce top-class scientists. As they always have done, scientists will play the lead role in helping address some of humanity's biggest challenges, be it future energy supply, global warming or starvation.

Finally, there is the matter of the contribution science makes to our economic prosperity. Industrial scientists apply their knowledge to invent products that individuals want to buy and which create wealth. If the UK is to retain its position as one of the world's leading economies, it needs to remain a competitive location for science-based industries like pharmaceuticals. This is especially true now, as a growing number of countries are producing world-class, highly-motivated scientists.

We all need scientists, which is why the teaching of science should matter to us all. It is for this reason that Pfizer is proud to be partnering with the Institute of Ideas to foster this series of essays by those, like ourselves, who are involved in and passionate about the future of science education in the UK. Let the debate begin.

INTRODUCTION

Tony Gilland

Science and society director, Institute of Ideas

Science and education have been areas of central concern to the work of the Institute of Ideas since its inception in 2000. We are therefore delighted to publish David Perks' essay *What is science education for?* and the associated responses, coming from a wide range of individuals concerned about the current state and future direction of science education in the UK.

All contributors to this publication agree that science education is in need of serious improvement. For some the overriding concern is the drastic decline in the numbers of students taking up physics and chemistry beyond GCSE level, and what this means for the future of education, commerce and scientific endeavour. For others it is a desire to provide students with a better understanding of basic scientific concepts in the context of contemporary philosophical, moral and sociopolitical debates about science. What priority should be attached to either of these objectives, and what approach should be taken to achieving them, is hotly contested within these pages.

Since this publication was conceived a year ago, the perceived crisis in science education has moved up the public agenda. From the threatened closure of Sussex University's chemistry department in early 2006, to the work of Alan Smithers and Pamela Robinson at Buckingham University highlighting the terminal decline of physics education, to the introduction of a new compulsory science curriculum for 14- to 16-year-olds, science education has been grabbing its share of the headlines. At the time of going to press, Reading University's Senior Management Board had just proposed to close the physics department by 2010.

Many have decried the current situation. The Royal Society, in partnership with other learned societies, teachers and science organisations, recently launched an initiative (Science Community Partnership Supporting Education) to address problems such as the declining numbers of young people taking A level physics and chemistry and the shortage of specialist teachers in these subjects. However, from a series of seminars and debates organised by the Institute of Ideas from April to June 2006, it was clear that many individuals with a direct interest in science education – teachers, students, industrialists, university scientists – had very different perspectives on what trends were shaping science education within schools, where the problems might lie and how the situation might be improved. The purpose of this publication is to clarify some of these points of difference, and from there to generate a wide-ranging public debate on what we should expect from science education.

From Gerry Lawless, head of chemistry at Sussex University, who successfully fought the closure of his department in 2006, to Sir Richard Sykes, Mary Warnock, Simon Singh and Michael Reiss, the new director of education at the Royal Society, we are delighted that so many eminent individuals have contributed to this publication. I would like to thank them, and I hope reading their thoughtful responses to David Perks' essay spurs many more people to join the debate.

A few further thanks. To David Perks, Claire Fox and other members of the Institute of Ideas' Education Forum, whose passion for debate and scrutiny of educational issues and developments provided the groundwork and much of the inspiration for this project. To Pfizer, and in particular Eliot Forster, Joel Morris, Jean Bradbury and John Coad, for having the foresight and courage to work in partnership with the Institute of Ideas on this. And to Jennie Bristow, Isobell Cripps, Trude Diesen, Joe Ewart, Waheeda Rahman and Brenda Stones, whose input and skills have helped to take these ideas into print.

Tony Gilland, October 2006

WHAT IS SCIENCE EDUCATION FOR?

David Perks

Many agree that something needs to be done to salvage science education in the UK. A recent study by Professor Alan Smithers and Dr Pamela Robinson revealed that the number of pupils studying A-level physics has fallen by 35 per cent since 1990.[1] According to their study the trend is even more dramatic in state schools. Within higher education (HE), the furore over the loss of university science departments reached a crescendo in March 2006, when Sussex University threatened its chemistry department with closure. As Peter Atkins, professor of chemistry at Oxford University, wrote in the *Times Higher Educational Supplement*:

> 'How can a vice-chancellor worth his salt take one of the UK's great chemistry departments and stamp it out like an academic cockroach? How many Nobel prize-winners would it need to have before it is seen to be worth hanging on to? Why kill a department that has one of the highest research ratings in the country?'[2]

Chemistry at Sussex was eventually given a reprieve after its head of department, Dr Gerry Lawless, fought a hard battle, resulting in a merger with biochemistry. But still the plight of the sciences seems dire: to the point where John Cridland, deputy director of the Confederation of British Industry (CBI), recently claimed: 'We are beginning to see UK companies saying it makes economic sense to source science graduates internationally, particularly from China and India.'[3] The CBI's director general, Richard Lambert, has identified the lack of specialist physics and chemistry teachers – only one in five science teachers has a specialist physics qualification, and one in four chemistry teachers has a specialist chemistry qualification – as a key cause for concern. Lambert warned that the government 'must set itself more challenging targets', and argued: 'we need more specialised teachers to share their enthusiasm for science and fire the imaginations of pupils, and to persuade them to study the core individual disciplines to high levels'.[4]

Science minister Lord Sainsbury, speaking to the Royal Society during Science Week in March 2006, attempted to put a gloss on the situation by pointing out that the number of graduates in computer science, medicine, and biological science were all up over the last decade. However, he had to concede that the number of engineering and technology graduates had fallen by 10 per cent, and graduates in physical sciences by 11 per cent, in the same decade.[5]

1   *Physics in schools and universities 2: Patterns and Policies,* Alan Smithers and Pamela Robinson, Centre for Education and Employment, University of Buckingham, August 2006
http://www.buckingham.ac.uk/education/research/ceer/pdfs/physicsprint-2.pdf

2   'Stop counting beans, start planting trees', Peter Atkins, *Times Higher Educational* Supplement, 17 March 2006

3   'UK looking overseas for science graduates', *Education Guardian,* 15 March 2006

4   'UK's World Class Science Base Under Threat as Young People Turn Their Back on Science', CBI Press Release, 14 August 2006

5   Presentation given by Lord Sainsbury, March 2006
http://www.royalsoc.ac.uk/page.asp?tip=1&id=4207

The UK government published its *Science and Innovation Framework 2004-2014: next steps*[6] document as part of the Budget in March 2006. The report acknowledges the worrying situation with regard to the uptake of A-level physics and chemistry, and warns: 'Declining science A-level entries have repercussions on the numbers studying science at HE. For example, those graduating with an undergraduate degree in chemistry fell by 27 per cent between 1994/95 and 2001/02, and by a further 7 per cent between 2002/03 and 2004/05.'

Certainly, the government's desire to encourage more young people to go on to study the physical sciences at school and university is welcome; and the report makes a number of interesting suggestions as to how this situation can be improved. For example, the government makes a commitment to secure more physics and chemistry teachers through a drive to 'recruit science graduates into teaching via Employment Based Routes with new incentives to providers of £1,000 per recruit'. It also specifies ambitious goals for the number of pupils going on to study physics, chemistry and mathematics at A-level by the year 2014. One of the more interesting suggestions put forward is that by 2008 there should be an entitlement to study separate sciences at GCSE if a pupil achieves level 6 by the end of key stage 3. (Students are assessed at age 14 on a scale of 1 to 8, and the majority achieve level 5 or 6.)

However, given the drastic shortage of specialist science teachers, the fact that only about one in eight science teacher trainees is a physics graduate[7], and the declining number of students taking the physical sciences at degree level, fulfilling these commitments is a major undertaking. For example, the government has already indicated that provision of an entitlement to study three separate sciences at GCSE will require 'collaborative arrangements with other schools, FE colleges and universities'[8], suggesting that many students will have to travel to other institutions to receive a thorough science education.

This is the context in which a major reform of GCSE science education, which enforces the compulsory study of 'scientific literacy', is now being introduced. From September 2006 all state school pupils at key stage 4 (aged 14-16) must be taught ideas about how science works in general – such as the nature of scientific evidence, the limitations of scientific evidence, and the social and ethical issues raised by science – alongside a broad appreciation of 'organisms and health, chemical and material behaviour, energy, electricity

6 *Science and Innovation Framework 2004-2014: next steps*, HM Treasury, 22 March 2006
   http://www.hm-treasury.gov.uk/media/D2E/4B/bud06_science_332v1.pdf

7 *Physics in schools and universities 2: Patterns and Policies*, Alan Smithers and Pamela Robinson, Centre for Education and Employment, University of Buckingham, August 2006
   http://www.buckingham.ac.uk/education/research/ceer/pdfs/physicsprint-2.pdf

8 *Science and Innovation Framework 2004-2014: next steps*, HM Treasury, 22 March 2006

and radiations, and the environment, Earth and universe'.[9] A range of new GCSE courses that meet these statutory requirements has been produced by the major exam boards in preparation for September 2006, and other qualifications such as BTEC diplomas have also been accredited.

The new science GCSEs have already attracted negative media coverage, with stories of independent schools abandoning them for the more traditional, subject-based international GCSEs; and much criticism has been made of two exam boards, Edexcel and AQA, for making their examination questions solely multiple choice.[10] However, what is most striking about the reform is the justification given for it. The reason given for the change is a desire to empower students as future citizens and consumers of science, rather than to train them as future scientists – the *producers* of science. On the face of it, this motivation appears to be at odds with the desire to ensure a major increase in the number of students taking physics and chemistry at A-level and degree level. As Ken Boston, chief executive of the Qualifications and Curriculum Authority (QCA), the public body responsible for the national curriculum, argued when announcing the curriculum change: 'Previous key stage 4 curricula were criticised for concentrating too much on the needs of future scientists at the expense of science that is relevant to students' everyday lives.'[11]

My argument is that we have arrived at a confused and contradictory situation that threatens to undermine our ability to deliver what so many people say we need: many more students studying science to a higher level. This situation has not come out of the blue, but is the product of trends that have been developing for some time. These include:

- 'Student-centred' educational approaches leading to constant attempts to make study more 'relevant' to students' immediate lives;
- An underestimation of the capabilities of students and a desire to protect them from failure, leading to the breaking down of subjects into 'bite-sized' chunks of digestible information at the expense of a deeper appreciation of the subjects as a whole;
- The decline of practical work and laboratory experiments;
- A disregard for the integrity of subject knowledge and an associated attempt to sideline teachers as 'knowledge intermediaries';
- Misplaced and exaggerated expectations about the role education can play in relation to wider social concerns;

9   *Programme of study: science, Key stage 4*, QCA, 2006 **http://www.qca.org.uk/downloads/10340_science_prog_of_study_from_2006_ks4.pdf**

10   For example see 'Top independent school to ditch GCSE science', Rebecca Smithers, *Guardian*, 3 September 2005; and 'Pass this GCSE without writing a word', Liz Lightfoot, *Daily Telegraph*, 10 June 2006

11   *Science: Changes to the curriculum from 2006 for Key Stage 4*, Foreword by Ken Boston, QCA, 2005

- Confusion about what science has to offer society.

The impact of these broad trends on science education in schools is the focus of this essay.

SCIENCE FOR CITIZENSHIP?

The critical question posed at the centre of recent educational reforms is: Should science education be aimed at the citizen or at the future scientist? The authors of the seminal report *Beyond 2000*, which paved the way for the introduction of the new compulsory science GCSE, were clear about their view that the training of future scientists has weighed too heavily on the teaching of science in the past:

> 'This report is the product of a desire to provide a new vision of an education in science for our young people. It is driven by a sense of a growing disparity between the science education provided in our schools and the needs and interests of the young people who will be our future citizens...Our view is that the form of science education we currently offer to young people is outmoded, and fundamentally is still a preparatory education for our future scientists...the ever-growing importance of scientific issues in our daily lives demands a populace who have sufficient knowledge and understanding to follow science and scientific debates with interest, and to engage with the issues science and technology poses – both for them individually, and for our society as a whole.'[12]

Many of those who are concerned about the training of future scientists, including the government, are equally concerned about the engagement of the populace with science and the issues it generates. As prime minister Tony Blair said in his speech to the Royal Society in 2002, 'science is vital to our country's continued future prosperity'.[13] Blair's speech recognised not only the threat posed to the UK's position in the world by the declining number of graduates in the physical sciences, but also the threat posed by the erosion of trust in science and government. This was at the time brought sharply into focus by public hostility to genetically modified (GM) crops: summed up in Blair's assertion that people outside Britain think we are 'completely overrun by protestors and pressure groups who use emotion to drive out reason'.[14]

12 *Beyond 2000*, Robin Millar and Jonathan Osborne, King's College, London, 1998 http://www.kcl.ac.uk/ education/publications/ bey2000.pdf

13 Tony Blair, Speech to the Royal Society, 23 May 2002 http://politics.guardian.co.uk/ speeches/story/ 0,11126,721029,00.html

14 *ibid.*

Given the broader uncertainty over how to handle public concerns about different aspects of science, from the MMR vaccination to animal experiments to nuclear power, it is not surprising that many are attracted by the idea of using education to solve the problem. But will it work? And what does politicising science education, through an increasing focus on issues and controversies, mean for the content of the education that students receive?

For those at the forefront of science education reform, public distrust of science seems to provide an opportunity as well as a problem. It is, they argue, by situating science education within the context of controversial debates that young people can make sense of science. As the authors of the Teaching and Learning Research Programme (TLRP) commentary *Science education in schools* claim: 'Research suggests that context-led courses lead to greater student interest, a greater appreciation of the relevance of learning to everyday life, and no measurable decrease in student understanding of science content.'[15]

The 'context-led' approach is driven by the presumed need to make science education relevant to the ordinary citizen, rather than the potential future scientist. As the report argues: 'We believe the best way forward is to provide the highest grade of 'science education for citizenship' for all students.'[16] The authors go on to assert that young people who do well on such a course 'will be increasingly motivated to follow science-related careers'. Despite this upbeat assessment of the 'context-led' approach, however, the authors concede that: 'The evidence that this approach results in an increased uptake of more advanced courses is less strong.'[17]

So what evidence is there that promoting 'science education for citizenship' to a central place in the curriculum will fulfil the twin goals of engaging the interests of students in science and producing more science graduates?

Already a pilot study, commissioned by the QCA, has been in operation since September 2003. The pilot study, Twenty First Century Science, is run by a consortium including the examining board OCR (Oxford, Cambridge and RSA Examinations), York University Education Group and the Nuffield Curriculum Centre. The Twenty First Century Science pilot GCSE courses have been run at 75 schools but have yet to be fully evaluated; three independent evaluations of the courses are expected to conclude their findings towards the end of 2006.

15   *Science education in schools: Issues, evidence and proposals,* TLRP, 2006 p.9

16   *ibid.* p.4

17   *ibid.* p.9

In February 2005 the QCA published the results of an initial and general evaluation of the Twenty First Century Science courses that it had undertaken.[18] This evaluation consisted of one consultant visiting seven of the 75 participating pilot centres during the first year of teaching the courses, and analysis of a postal evaluation questionnaire completed by teachers at 40 of the centres at the end of the first year of teaching.

This provisional evaluation provides weak evidence that the Twenty First Century Science courses will lead to an increased uptake in students studying science beyond GCSE. The questionnaire evaluation found 'a significant minority of respondents (12 centres; 30 per cent) reported that no more students than usual had indicated they would take science subjects beyond GCSE' (*emphasis in original*); 20 per cent reported '**some more**' or a '**few more**' students 'had confirmed an intention to progress to post-16 science studies', and 7.5 per cent stated that 'the pilot courses had resulted in there being **fewer** than normal students wishing to progress on to post-16 studies'. The remainder were unable to answer the question for one reason or another.

However, on the other key question of concern – engagement – the evaluation found that schools and students were generally positive about the courses with 'a significant majority (33 out of the 40 centres; 82.5 per cent) of the pilot centres' reporting that they 'would recommend the pilot science GCSEs to other teachers/centres'. One primary reason given for this was that the course content was 'more relevant and up-to-date and avoids primarily targeting the needs and interests of students intending to progress on to AS/A-level science courses'. The major criticism of the courses from teachers and students was the lack of practical activity.

Given the inherent limitations of a brief evaluation of the first year of the pilot courses, it is surprising that the QCA chose not to wait for the results of the three independent reviews of Twenty First Century Science before turning major elements of the pilot courses into a new programme of study shaping the future content of compulsory science GCSEs. Surely it would have been more productive to allow time for the results of these evaluations to have been disseminated and discussed widely?

18   *Evaluation and analysis of the science for the 21st Century pilot GCSEs*, QCA, February 2005

Indeed, following a debate about the new GCSEs organised by the Institute of Ideas in June 2006, Andrew Hunt, a co-director of the Twenty First Century Science project, questioned whether a course in scientific literacy should be a compulsory component of a science GCSE, arguing: 'No one science course is right for everyone. No one approach engages all young people appropriately to allow them to learn science successfully.'[19] Robin Millar, another co-director of the project, is explicit that Twenty First Century Science is 'clearly not the only form that a scientific literacy course for this age level could take'.[20]

So why rush through such a radical change to the science curriculum, especially when we have little evidence that such a major change in direction will influence the key problem of the declining uptake of the physical sciences in schools and universities?

This shift towards promoting 'scientific literacy' over science itself is the result of deeper trends in the reform of science education, and education as a whole, which have already led to conflicting demands being placed upon the science curriculum, assessment procedures and science teachers.

MAKING SCIENCE 'RELEVANT'

One of the major demands made of education in recent years has been to make school subjects more 'relevant' to pupils. School children, it is argued, cannot be expected to engage with concepts and ideas beyond their immediate frame of reference: educationalists, therefore, should relate the subjects they teach directly to the language and ideas with which pupils are familiar in their everyday lives. It is not just educationalists who have adopted this patronising approach towards young people. The Church of England, for example, in 2005 announced plans to hold services everywhere from skateboarding parks to pubs and cafes. Not to be outdone, the Duke of Edinburgh's Award came up with slogans such as 'NE14 Fun?', 'Wanna Feel Gr8?' and 'Boréd? U Wont B' in an attempt to speak to young people with 'a different voice'.[21]

The demands of 'relevance' have attracted some criticism in other disciplines. As the columnist Martin Samuel argued in *The Times* about a revision guide on Shakespeare that attempted to translate the Bard's words into teenage street-speak:

'Instead of attempting to engage the class in the work of a genius who brought such richness to our language, the entry level for the modern student is now crass and

19 'Science Issues, Claire Fox and her case against the changes to GCSE Science', Andrew Hunt, Nuffield Curriculum Centre website, 14 July 2006 **http://www.nuffieldcurriculum centre.org/go/ CurriculumIssues/ Issue_333.html**

20 'Twenty First Century Science: Insights from the design and implementation of a scientific literacy approach in school science', Robin Millar, *International Journal of Science Education* (in press). Forthcoming, 2006

21 'Hey, Miss, this homework just ain't relevant', Claire Fox, *The Times*, 22 October 2005

unsophisticated. Instead of trying to shake future generations out of complacency, their ignorance and lack of interest is presumed. We no longer aspire to education but to maintenance. We babysit, really, until *X Factor* begins. We depict Shakespeare as boring and obscure, then wonder why teenagers produce exam papers full of gibberish and misunderstanding.'[22]

But it would seem the same disease of 'dumbing down' in the name of relevance has afflicted science education without attracting such concerns. The House of Commons Science and Technology Select Committee report, *Science education from 14 to 19*, published in 2002, decried the double science GCSE which most students now study from 14 to 16, where all three sciences are studied together and awarded two equal GCSE grades. There are many valid criticisms to be made of double science. However, the Commons Select Committee's concern was primarily with its over-emphasis on scientific facts rather than cultural relevance:

'The GCSE science curriculum is over-prescriptive. This puts students off science because they do not have the flexibility to explore areas which interest them. It kills the interest in science which may have been kindled at primary school.'[23]

Sir Gareth Roberts was commissioned by the government in 2001 to review the supply of science and engineering skills. His influential report, known as the Roberts Review, recommended that the curriculum should be reformed with the aim of 'improving the relevance of the science curriculum to pupils in order to capture the interests of pupils (especially girls) and to better enthuse and equip them to study science (particularly the physical sciences) at higher level'.[24]

Much has been made of a widely-quoted survey of A-level science students carried out by the Science Museum in 2002.[25] According to the survey, over half of students who studied double science GCSE felt it failed to make them 'curious about the world'. The survey found that most young people wanted more relevant and contemporary science, especially controversial issues. Nearly half of the respondents claimed that discussion and debate in class was the most useful way of learning science.

What surprises me is not the fact that students complain about learning science – it was

22 'Romeo, wherefore art thou talking stupid?' *The Times*, 6 June 2006

23 *Science Education from 14 to 19*, House of Commons Science and Technology Committee, Third Report of Session 2001-02, Volume I, p.15

24 The Roberts Review, *SET for Success*, 2002, HM Treasury, p.6 http://www.hm-treasury.gov.uk/media/643/FB/ACF11FD.pdf

25 Cerini, B., Murray, I. and Reiss, M., 'Student Review of the Science Curriculum: Major Findings', Planet Science, London (2003) Available at http://www.planet-science.com/sciteach/review/Findings.pdf

DO WE REALLY WANT TO HAND OVER CONTROL OF THE CURRICULUM TO TEENAGERS?

ever thus – but that today we take them seriously. Children are prone to dislike being told to do anything that demands effort from them, as any teacher or parent will confirm. It is only after they have gained something from the experience that they are going to feel any gratitude for the effort adults put into helping them achieve it.

However, something different happens if we, as educators, take pupils' complaints about science lessons on board. This brings into question the whole enterprise of trying to educate young people about science. If the children get wind of our defensiveness then they will question the purpose and value of science education still more.

There is a long tradition of educational research looking at why pupils find science hard to learn.[26] Cultural explanations for this phenomenon centre on a failure to connect with the student during the science lesson.[27] The authors of the TLRP commentary *Science education in schools* explain it like this:

> 'There can be substantial discontinuities between what young people experience in their school science lessons and in the rest of their lives.'[28]

The authors go on to argue: 'Unless school science explicitly engages with the enthusiasms and concerns of...students, it will lose their interest.'

This outlook leads to the call to listen to the 'student's voice' within the classroom. As the report puts it, 'science education can only succeed when students believe that the science they are being taught is of personal worth to themselves'. But this sounds like a call to ask the students what they would like to do in their science lessons. Do we really want to hand over control of the curriculum to teenagers?

The focusing of the curriculum on controversial aspects of the implementation of science and technology, such as genetic modification or nuclear power, can no doubt provide young people with opportunity to express themselves about issues we all face. But in the absence of a thorough grasp of science and a clear understanding of its importance in the context of a particular debate, any discussion will quickly boil down to rhetorical posturing or simply confusion. Asking teenagers to make up their minds about anything is pretty daunting. But

26 *Young people's images of science*, Rosalind Driver, John Leach, Robin Millar and Phil Scott, Oxford University Press, 1996

27 'Science education: Border crossing into the subculture of science', Glen Aikenhead, in *Studies in Science Education*, vol. 27, 1996, pp.1-52

28 *Science education in schools: Issues, evidence and proposals*, TLRP, 2006, p.5

if you try to ask them to decide if we need to replace the UK's nuclear power stations, you are far more likely to get the question: 'Sir, what is nuclear power?'

There is a paradox at the heart of the debate about making science more relevant to young people. Science is widely regarded as fascinating outside of school science lessons. The sales of popular science books like Bill Bryson's *A Short History of Nearly Everything*, and the audience for TV programmes like Sky's *Brainiac Science Abuse*, indicate that science is of great interest to young people. Young people have a profound interest in what science can tell them about themselves and the world around them. Whether it is the nature of evolution and the relationship between science and religion or our understanding of the history of the universe, every child is fascinated by their relationship to science.

But we don't need to flatter young people by asking them what they think about these issues. We do need to help them learn as much as they can about science, so that they can understand what science tells them about the natural world and their place in it. Where we have failed is in not translating this thirst for knowledge into more students choosing a serious academic study of the sciences, which would ultimately help all of us to come closer to answering some of these questions.

IS SCIENCE TOO HARD?

'School science can be so boring it puts young people off science for life.'[29]

This was how Dr Ian Gibson, then Chairman of the House of Commons Science and Technology Committee, in 2002 explained the failure to attract more young people towards science. Gibson continued: 'GCSE science students have to cram in so many facts that they have no time to explore interesting ideas.' Robin Millar and Jonathan Osborne make the same point in Beyond 2000, claiming that the curriculum presents science as 'a succession of 'facts' to be learnt, with insufficient indication of any overarching coherence and a lack of contextual relevance to the future needs of young people'.[30]

29 'Science lessons tedious and dull', *BBC News*, 11 July 2002

30 *Beyond 2000*, Robin Millar and Jonathan Osborne, King's College, London, 1998, p.4

Nobody has ever claimed that science is an easy discipline to master. But in the contemporary period science education is portrayed from all quarters as the rote learning of disconnected dry facts – so much so that even the QCA celebrates the emphasis on

'TRADITIONAL' SCIENCE TEACHING IS NOT JUST A PROCESS OF ASKING PUPILS TO MEMORISE FACTS

'reduced content and factual recall'[31] in its new programme of study for key stage 4. This is leading to a fundamental redefinition of what science education is.

Millar argues that 'what citizens require is a broad, qualitative grasp of the major science explanations; the detail which many students find off-putting is rarely needed'.[32] The Twenty First Century Science pilot focuses instead on a cultural appreciation of the important stories or 'science explanations'.

According to Millar, selecting which 'science explanations' to include in the curriculum is a matter of looking at what a scientifically literate citizen ought to know about science. For Millar, the choice of which 'science explanations' to include must take seriously 'the kind of science that people encounter through the news media'. Unsurprisingly, health and medicine figure more prominently under these criteria than elementary physics or chemistry. It seems rather odd that, in putting the case for a new curriculum, Millar is prepared to argue that the mass media should have a more decisive influence on deciding the nature of the science curriculum than the intellectual integrity of the subject.

But the key problem with this approach is its assumption that 'traditional' science teaching is just a process of asking pupils to copy and memorise facts. This belittles the effort that goes into teaching pupils to grasp what amounts to a highly abstract and difficult way of thinking about nature. Learning the sciences presents considerable challenges to young people. The role of the teacher in this is continually to challenge preconceived notions, and present new ways of thinking about the subject.

Mastery on the part of the pupil involves acquiring factual knowledge and building models to incorporate this knowledge. As children progress they begin to realise that the models they have been taught are insufficient and need to be replaced, to accommodate the new facts they are meeting about the way nature behaves. As well as refining the models they use to describe nature, students gradually become conscious of what it means to build and try out new models themselves. All the time they need to be confronted with the need to test their ideas against experimental evidence. Facilitating this process over a period of time is not the same as getting students to rote-learn dry facts. It is a question of constructing the capacity for abstract thought.

31 QCA presentation on changes in 2006
http://www.qca.org.uk/downloads/14008_presentation_changes_to_Science_June_2005.ppt

32 'Twenty First Century Science: Insights from the design and implementation of a scientific literacy approach in school science', Robin Millar, *International Journal of Science Education* (in press). Forthcoming, 2006, p.13

The accepted critique of 'traditional' science teaching is a shallow pastiche of the truth, and only serves to flatter the new thinking about science education. Science teaching is much more than either passing on the rote-learning of disembodied theory or the stories about science that are now being prescribed. It is about treating students as potential future scientists and providing them with the foundations of a scientific understanding of the world that will stand them in good stead whether they pursue science further or not.

BITE-SIZED CHUNKS

The extent to which educationalists have become despondent about the possibility and worth of attempting to provide students with such an opportunity to master the sciences is well reflected by the modularisation of courses and associated assessment methods.

The introduction of modular A-levels in 2000 was a major shift in the method of assessment of the sciences in schools. The split between AS and A2 examinations in the first and second year of A-levels, which went alongside modularisation, hid a further change: the lowering of the standard expected during the first year of the course to a point between GCSE and A-level. Add to this the possibility of retaking modules within the A-level course repeatedly over its duration, and the credibility of the final grades achieved is inevitably reduced.

As reported in *The Sunday Times* in December 2005, a large number of independent schools have been seriously considering abandoning the state A-level system in favour of a tougher qualification. Ralph Townsend, head of Winchester, said: 'We are concerned about the reduction in academic rigour at A-level. We want to move away from courses designed in bite-sized chunks that lack cohesion.'[33]

The triple award, or separate science examinations, offered by all the examining boards until the summer of 2006, still offered a terminal examination. However, alongside the introduction of the new programme of study for science, the QCA has seen fit to enforce the modularisation of all science GCSE examinations – including the separate science GCSEs. All the same arguments about fragmenting the courses and over-examining pupils are now set to resurface in the one part of the school system that had avoided these problems. In addition, there is to be a greater emphasis on coursework, which is set to rise

33 'Top private schools to drop 'easy' A-levels', *The Sunday Times*, 11 December 2005

from 20 per cent to 33 per cent under the new specifications – meaning that pupils will necessarily experience a greater assessment burden.

As made clear by the Roberts Review in 2002, students find it hard to make the progression from GCSE to A-level in the physical sciences because of the increased demands placed on the students. The changes being brought in at GCSE are likely to compromise still further the chances of students succeeding, by diluting the rigour of assessment procedures.

Sitting a single examination at the end of a two-year course may seem like a daunting prospect for a teenager, but it can provide the pressure and focus to make learning a subject meaningful. Pupils who currently sit modules in GCSE double science often have little or no idea of the examination process and find it hard to compartmentalise knowledge for each separate modular examination. With pupils sitting strings of modules at different times during the year with little idea of how they contribute to their actual qualifications, the whole process becomes an administrative nightmare. A single terminal examination, by contrast, asks pupils to raise their game at a well-defined and pivotal moment in their school career. This pressure forces both the pupils and their teachers to consolidate their understanding of the subject, and gives pupils a chance to get to grips with the intellectual integrity of the subject as a whole. The chances of this happening with a modular scheme of assessment are heavily reduced.

Teaching separate sciences has much to offer both teachers and pupils, because it promotes subject specialists who love their discipline and can transmit their passion and knowledge through to their pupils. I have previously argued that if parents want to know how to spot a good state school, they should simply ask whether the school teaches separate science subjects.[34]

In this context we should surely be concerned about the growing gulf between the education on offer within the independent sector compared to that in many state schools. As Boris Johnson has argued in the *Observer*: 'We are staring at a growing social iniquity that some testing academic subjects are being ghettoised in the independent sector and grammar schools.'[35] This bleak statement echoes the conclusion drawn by Professor Alan Smithers and Dr Pamela Robinson about the possible demise of physics as a subject within the state sector.[36]

34 'Let's get physical', David Perks, *spiked*, 11 September 2003

35 A teaching scandal we can't afford', Boris Johnson, *Observer*, 9 July 2006

36 *Physics in schools and colleges: Teacher Deployment and Student Outcomes*, Alan Smithers and Pamela Robinson, Centre for Education and Employment, University of Buckingham, November 2005, p.iv **http://www.buckingham.ac.uk/ education/research/ceer/pdfs/ physicsprint.pdf**

It was reported in August 2005 that 15 independent schools were planning to reject the new science GCSE. According to Dr Martin Stephen, High Master of St Paul's School in London, this was on the basis that it had 'a terrifying absence of proper science'.[37] It should be of real concern to us if the independent sector thinks the new GCSEs will undermine the chances of its pupils taking science seriously.

The creation of a kind of educational apartheid is likely to be further accelerated by the adoption of the new science GCSEs. If science education is to prosper post-16, schools are going to be forced to make hard choices. Do they give students the demanding option of three separate sciences, or do they opt for the more 'relevant' suite of Twenty First Century Science courses? Under pressure to meet GCSE grade targets in order to justify specialist school status, even good schools in the state sector will think twice before offering the separate sciences.

The new science GCSEs, with their emphasis on 'scientific literacy', can only result in a negative downward pressure on the uptake of the physical sciences at both A-level and undergraduate level for pupils from state schools.

THE DEATH OF THE EXPERIMENTAL METHOD?

'Are we about to say goodbye to the white coat and science laboratory in schools?'[38] I wrote in the *Times Educational Supplement* earlier in 2006. We have already seen the invasion of the ubiquitous interactive whiteboard as the new stock in trade of most secondary school science teachers. There is great pressure on science teachers to turn to PowerPoint presentations or playing DVDs rather than doing experiments. If there is one thing that gives credence to the idea that science education involves learning too many dry facts, it is surely this trend. Unfortunately the emphasis on 'scientific literacy' seems to be exacerbating the situation.

This is all the more confusing when experimental work remains a very popular aspect of science lessons. NESTA, the National Endowment for Science, Technology and the Arts, conducted a recent study on how the manner in which children are taught science affects their learning. A major conclusion drawn from the study backs up the point that too much science is being taught as just facts on a board, rather than '... a glorious exploration of the

37 "At least 15 schools to snub GCSE science exam', *Independent*, 6 August 2005

38 'Dark forces in the lab', David Perks, *Times Educational Supplement*, 6 January 2006

THE DECLINE IN THE PRACTICAL ELEMENT OF SCIENCE TEACHING IS NO ACCIDENT OR OVERSIGHT

unknown through practical experimentation'. As the authors go on to say: 'lessons are now too much based around books and not enough around Bunsen Burners'.[39]

Even the Science Museum survey previously discussed gave a huge thumbs-up to practical work, with 79 per cent of science students claiming it helped them to understand their science. So it would seem logical to think that the new approach to science teaching should take account of the need to reinstate the importance of practical work in science lessons. However, those at the forefront of reforming science education seem to have drawn the opposite conclusion.

Derek Bell, chief executive of the Association for Science Education and a prominent supporter of the new science GCSE, said when giving evidence to the 2002 Commons Select Committee report on *Science education from 14 to 19*: 'There is a great danger of being conned into [thinking that] the answer to it all is doing more practical work. Doing practical work in itself is not going to help children learn more effectively or motivate them.'[40] But why should the proponents of educational reforms turn away from practical work? It would seem to fly in the face of the views of the students, and the experience of most teachers.

In fact, the biggest criticism the Twenty First Century Science pilot courses received from participating teachers after its first year was the lack of practical work. As one teacher put it: 'The lack of practical activities led to pupils being 'turned off'.'[41] Millar himself conceded: 'If "scientific literacy" courses allocate more time to discussion of issues and analysis of data and arguments, this may inevitably impact on the time available for practical activities.'[42]

However, the decline in the practical element of science teaching is no accident or oversight. Rather, the philosophy behind the new approach to science teaching is to emphasise the pupil as a consumer of science, not as a potential scientist. The skills associated with being 'scientifically literate' are far more closely related to textual analysis and data interpretation than to experimental skills.

This is not only true of the pilot study. The new QCA programme of study for science at key

39 *A Mission for Innovation – Fostering science enquiry learning across the UK*, Jonathan Kestenbaum, CEO of NESTA, 2006
http://www.nesta.org.uk/ inspireme/think_jk_june06. html

40 *Science Education from 14 to 19*, House of Commons Science and Technology Committee, Third Report of Session 2001-02, vol. I, p.20

41 'Twenty First Century Science: Insights from the design and implementation of a scientific literacy approach in school science', Robin Millar, *International Journal of Science Education* (in press). Forthcoming, 2006

42 *ibid.*

stage 4 (GCSE) makes explicit in 'how science works' the kind of skills that are important to a scientifically literate citizen. Under the section 'Practical and Enquiry Skills', we can see that the laboratory experiment has been displaced by 'problem-solving and enquiry skills'. Other aspects highlighted, aside from a reference to safety issues when collecting first-hand data, focus primarily on data collection and evaluation, not experimental work. There is an emphasis on using 'secondary sources, including using ICT sources and tools'. The level of complexity involved in appreciating the experimental method is far below that acknowledged previously at key stage 4. The best that is put forward is the vague 'plan to test a scientific idea, answer a scientific question or solve a scientific problem'. The final element of this section gives the game away, by emphasising how pupils 'evaluate methods of collection of data and consider their validity and reliability as evidence' – in other words, discussion of scientific methods and their validity is privileged over conducting experiments.

In the context of relating 'their understanding of science to their own and others' decisions about lifestyles and to scientific and technological developments in society'[43], it is hard to escape the conclusion that what is being asked of young people is to assess conflicting opinions in the media rather than carry out experiments. In fact, the coursework components offered by the GCSE examination boards veer towards writing balanced arguments about science in the news, rather than carrying out a practical investigation.

Additionally, the emphasis on dealing with science in the context of health issues means a subtle shift in the version of science that is being presented to young people. The controlled laboratory experiment – the backbone of modern scientific enquiry – is being replaced by the field study.

The controlled laboratory experiment is the approach used to reduce scientific problems down to their simplest components and discover the laws that govern the behaviour of those components. This approach is the source of science's greatest discoveries. By comparison, the field trial of a new drug is a much less certain approach to scientific enquiry. Statistical correlations within a population, even with a control group, can only indicate a likely relationship between a new drug and an expected outcome. This is a far less powerful model of experimental science than laboratory science.

43 *Programme of study: science, Key stage 4*, QCA, 2006

THE CONTROLLED LABORATORY
EXPERIMENT IS BEING REPLACED BY
THE FIELD STUDY

The effect of sidelining the laboratory experiment within the curriculum in favour of epidemiology can only lead to a wider acceptance of the provisional character of scientific knowledge. Scientists in this description of science become just another pressure group clutching hold of empirical data to pursue their case. But the scientific method is about much more than crude empiricism. It is about the construction of a way of looking at nature that allows us to gain increasing certainty of our understanding through testing theories against experimental data.

WHAT ARE TEACHERS FOR?

Those on all sides of the debate about how we improve science education can perhaps agree on this: Teachers are the most vital asset in the project of educating the next generation. As the authors of *Science education in schools* put it:

'The teacher is the single most important source of variation in the quality of learning.'[44]

But as the Roberts Review pointed out back in 2002, there are serious concerns 'where science teachers are often required to teach areas of science that they did not study at degree level (nor, in many cases at A-level)'.[45] And as Boris Johnson argued in the *Observer* in July, 'it cannot be right that if you study physics in a state school, you only have a 29 per cent chance of being taught by someone with a degree in that subject'.[46]

Smithers and Robinson, in their study of the decline in physics in schools, make a clear correlation between having a well-qualified physics teacher and gaining good results:

'Teachers' expertise as measured by qualification is the second most powerful predictor of pupil achievement in GCSE and A-level physics after pupil ability.'[47]

As the government made clear in its document *Science and Innovation Framework 2004-2014: next steps*, any serious attempt to address the deficit in the physical sciences must consider providing an increase in well-qualified subject specialist teachers. However, this does not appear to be prominent amongst the concerns of those promoting education for

44 *Science education in schools: Issues, evidence and proposals,* TLRP, 2006, p.11

45 The Roberts Review, *SET for Success,* 2002, HM Treasury, p.4, paragraph 0.17

46 'A teaching scandal we can't afford', Boris Johnson, *Observer,* 9 July 2006

47 *Physics in schools and colleges: Teacher deployment and student outcomes,* Alan Smithers and Pamela Robinson, University of Buckingham, November 2005. Executive summary, p.i

'scientific literacy'.

ADVOCATES OF REFORM CELEBRATE THE SIDELINING OF TEACHERS' EXPERTISE

The concern of the educational reform lobby is not specialist subject knowledge but what is called 'pedagogical content knowledge', or PCK. This term refers to 'the best ways of teaching specific science content and concepts to particular groups of students'.[48] Unfortunately, this does not mean learning how to do exciting laboratory experiments and demonstrations. Instead, the focus of teacher training is being redirected towards learning the new content of the 'scientific literacy' curriculum and how best to communicate those ideas to students.

Ken Boston, chief executive of the QCA, makes the case that pupils need 'transferable skills to cope with changing demands'. He argues that we should teach 'the ability to argue, to develop theories...and to ask the right questions'[49] – as though such skills can be taught in the abstract, separated from the subject matter to which they relate.

Incredibly, rather than emphasising the need to revitalise subject specialist knowledge before entering the classroom, we are told that even teachers with a good science degree need to learn different skills and ideas. Science teachers will need to teach ideas like 'the nature, processes and practices of science', which have 'traditionally been implicit rather than explicit in professional development'. Realising the size of the task they have set themselves, the advocates of reform envisage inculcating this new approach amongst teachers through 'coaching by experts, with opportunities to reflect in collegial settings on changes in classroom practice'.

Such a re-education programme for science teachers is seen as central to the success of teaching for 'scientific literacy'. As the influential educationalist Jonathan Osborne puts it:

> '... this requires the teacher to see him/herself less as a transmitter of information, reliant on a closed authoritative dialogue, and more as a facilitator of opportunities which enable discursive consideration and exploration by students of the epistemic and cognitive dimensions of science.'[50]

According to this approach, teachers should become 'knowledge intermediaries' who provide opportunities for students to 'explore and reflect on ideas involved'. This is

48 *Science education in schools: Issues, evidence and proposals*, TLRP, 2006, p.12

49 'A catalyst for change in the school science', Ken Boston, *Daily Telegraph*, 8 March 2006

50 See *Teaching and Learning: Research Briefing No. 3*, June 2003

obviously rather different from the traditional view of a science teacher. Osborne goes on to say:

> 'Given that the subject-culture of science teaching is dominated by a view of science as a body of given knowledge, with little scope for argumentative discourse and where plural alternatives are rarely considered, the incorporation of 'ideas-about-science' poses a substantive challenge for the teaching of science.'[51]

By stressing the discursive nature of the new science education, the advocates of reform celebrate the sidelining of teachers' expertise in their subject. They locate the central educational experience within the dialogue between pupils and teachers, rather than in an engagement with the subject as a body of knowledge. Instead of teaching the patterns between elements in the periodic table, we are supposed to encourage pupils to discuss the motivations of the different parties involved in a topical health panic like that surrounding MMR.

The problem is starkly put by Smithers and Robinson in the case of physics teaching:

> 'Physics in schools is at risk both through redefinition and lack of teachers with expertise in the subject.'[52]

The advocates of reform may call for incentives to encourage science teachers to stay in the profession; but they are at the same time trying to turn science teachers into something they were never trained to be and in which they have no specialist knowledge. Even if the subject specialist teachers we all think we need do want to teach 'scientific literacy', it is unlikely that many will have more than the vaguest idea of how to teach or understand ethics, philosophy, media studies, cultural studies and sociology to any great depth. Asking good physics and chemistry graduates to re-train to attempt such an impossible task hardly seems the best way to make use of their knowledge and talents within the teaching profession.

CAN 'SCIENTIFIC LITERACY' REBUILD CIVIL SOCIETY?

Robin Millar and Jonathan Osborne made the case for a move towards teaching for 'scientific literacy' back in 1998, in their report *Beyond 2000*. They claim that 'our future

[51] *ibid.*

[52] *Physics in schools and colleges: Teacher Deployment and Student Outcomes,* Alan Smithers and Pamela Robinson, Centre for Education and Employment, University of Buckingham, November 2005, p.iv

society will need a larger number of individuals with a broader understanding of science both for work and to enable them to participate as citizens in a democratic society'.[53]

According to *Beyond 2000*, science education should focus on the consumer of science rather than the producer of science. Robin Millar argues that the aim of the Twenty First Century Science pilot is to create a '"critically aware" consumer'.[54] This is explicitly targeted at a perceived democratic deficit. As he puts it:

> 'For citizens, the need is to be able to live and act with reasonable comfort and confidence in a society that is deeply influenced and shaped by artefacts, ideas and values of science – rather than feeling excluded from a whole area of discourse, and hence marginalised.'[55]

Ken Boston, chief executive of the QCA, explains his concern 'that school science is not adequately preparing young people to arrive at informed opinions about current issues such as global climate change, the threat of a world-wide flu pandemic, the risks and benefits of nuclear power or the MMR vaccination'.[56]

To put it simply: the new science curriculum is trying to make up for the fact that politicians and scientists don't seem able to get their message across in the public arena. Teaching 'scientific literacy' is clearly seen as a counter-balance to media panics about MMR and bird flu.

Anyone who follows debates in education will be familiar with politicians' claims that education can solve every social ill imaginable. The difference in this case is that the claims are being made by people within education and not from outside. But is it sensible to base the case for educational reform on the claim that teaching 'scientific literacy' will help offset political problems?

Tony Blair is acutely aware of the dilemma politicians face when dealing with the public's attitude towards science. As he said back in 2002:

> '...Britain can benefit enormously from scientific advance. But precisely because the advances are so immense, people worry.'[57]

53 *Beyond 2000*, Robin Millar and Jonathan Osborne, King's College, London, 1998, p.8

54 'Twenty First Century Science: Insights from the design and implementation of a scientific literacy approach in school science', Robin Millar, *International Journal of Science Education* (in press). Forthcoming, 2006, p.18

55 *ibid*, p.8

56 'A catalyst for change in the school science', Ken Boston, *Daily Telegraph*, 8 March 2006

57 Tony Blair, Speech to the Royal Society, 23 May 2002

Worrying about scientific advance is nothing new. What makes our situation unique is the depth of our current propensity to see catastrophe in technological advance. There is a general defensiveness on the part of politicians when faced with decisions about the use of science and technology: look, for example, at their sensitivity to criticisms over the building of new nuclear power stations.

But teachers can no more deal with this than politicians. Expecting teachers to be able to turn children away from the concerns associated with nuclear power or growing GM crops is asking too much of education.

It does not help matters that the proponents of 'scientific literacy' view pupils as 'consumers of science' when dealing with complex ethical dilemmas. We are in danger of encouraging only a cursory engagement with the issues in order to emphasise instead the ability of pupils to make their own decisions. This is a caricature of democracy, never mind science. Instead of empowering young people as well-informed citizens, we run the risk of setting them afloat in a sea of ethical uncertainty, with no possibility of anchoring themselves to the certainties that a scientific body of knowledge can provide.

Ironically, this approach to teaching the scientific method is in danger of assuming a level of sophistication beyond most graduates, let alone 14-year-olds. Teenagers have a simple approach to education: they want to know what the answer is. Teachers supply students with the building blocks of knowledge, which act as a foundation for their understanding. If we think we can short-circuit this process we are mistaken. We may try to teach pupils a theoretical understanding of how scientists assess the risks associated with the introduction of new vaccinations, for example, but without a foundation of knowledge and understanding of the issues their understanding will be vastly over-simplified.

In trying to answer the question whether complementary medicine is a sensible way to treat patients, would young people be better off with a foundation in molecular chemistry or a crude version of epidemiology? Inevitably they will end up rote-learning curtailed and largely inappropriate explanations of scientific epistemology and public health policy, which will be of little use to them outside the classroom. Disembodied theory is even more useless than dry facts.

INTRODUCING A DISCUSSION ABOUT 'UNCERTAINTY' CAN EASILY COMPOUND PUPILS' FEARS ABOUT SCIENCE

Advocates of 'scientific literacy' go too far in claiming it can help rebuild civil society, and they underestimate the demands of debating the ethical and social complexities of contemporary scientific issues. But they have also allowed for a disturbing redefinition of the science to occur. There is a school of thought that sees science as an elitist paradigm. For example Dr Jerry Ravetz, author of *Scientific Knowledge and its Social Problems* and a witness to the 2002 Commons Select Committee report on *Science education from 14 to 19*, claimed: 'science education is one of the last surviving authoritarian social-intellectual systems in Europe'.[58]

Some within the academic community base their critique of science on the idea that knowledge is socially constructed. As a result of this perspective, it runs into conflict with science taught as objective fact rather than negotiated truth. Even though this perspective is not widely accepted within the scientific community, its influence has meant that there is defensiveness about making too strong a claim for scientific knowledge for fear of being branded elitist. Instead, both supporters and critics of science emphasise scientific 'uncertainty'. One side does so for fear of being labelled too arrogant, and the other side because it does not accept scientific objectivity.

Yet, as Sir Robert May, a former President of the Royal Society, has argued:

'At the ever expanding frontiers, different ideas and opinions contend; the terrain is bumpy. But there are huge swathes of territory behind the frontier where evidence-based understanding has been securely achieved. For example, the Laws of Thermodynamics tell us assuredly that perpetual motion machines are impossible. In astonishing defiance of intuition, we now know that mass and energy can be interchanged, according to science's most celebrated formula, $E = mc^2$.'[59]

In the context of classroom discussions of broad social concerns about science that have their own particular drivers, the focus on scientific 'uncertainty' over the vast body of knowledge that has been built up over time threatens to become a key feature of what many students will take from their experience of science education.

For example, one of the missing elements in understanding the collapse of the MMR

58 *Science Education from 14 to 19*, House of Commons Science and Technology Committee, Third Report of Session 2001-02, vol. I, p.16

59 'Threats to Tomorrow's World': President's Anniversary Address 2005, Lord Robert May of Oxford, Royal Society, 30 November 2005

vaccination programme in parts of the UK is that people's perceptions of risk are not solely related to their knowledge of the scientific evidence. General distrust of past authority figures, such as the medical establishment, and enthusiasm for the 'natural', as evidenced by the massive growth in the market for alternative medicines, are just two factors that have played a substantial role in influencing people's outlooks on such questions. Being complex and cultural in character, neither of these dynamics can be easily extinguished by the very certain scientific evidence about the absence of a link between the MMR vaccination and autism – other factors raise doubts in many people's minds about the validity of the evidence. This being the case in wider society there is no reason to think that things should be different within the classroom. Discussion of unresolved social issues like the MMR debate within the context of science classes for 14-16 year olds could easily generate real confusion about what is and is not scientifically known.

In this sense, introducing a discussion about scientific 'uncertainty' in the context of discussing controversies about science can easily compound pupils' fears about the use of science. If we don't trust what government and scientists tell us outside the classroom, are we likely suddenly to believe in it all when we go through the classroom doors? It is far more likely that teachers will meet the same general distrust of science within the classroom.

I very much doubt that studying 'scientific literacy' will either encourage young people to trust science in later life, or make them want to study it further at school and university. Yet the QCA has insisted that 'scientific literacy' is to become a mandatory aspect of every child's education at GCSE from September 2006. Where does this leave science education, now and in the future?

SCIENCE EDUCATION: SOME PRINCIPLES

In this essay I have tried to make clear that whilst many individuals and organisations are rightly concerned about the declining uptake of the physical sciences beyond GCSE and the lack of teachers with specialist qualifications in these subjects, few have grasped the confusing and contradictory trends that have been shaping science education for the last twenty years. At present, many seem to take the view that the new science GCSEs should be given a chance to demonstrate what impact they might have. Meanwhile, government promises of more subject specialist science teachers and access to the study of three separate science GCSEs for all students achieving level 6 at key stage 3 are laudable, but not yet very convincing.

The hope seems to be that somehow, through the current science education reforms, we will arrive at a situation where the general populace become less sceptical and prone to worry about issues related to science and technology, whilst at the same time more students are trained in the sciences to a high level and become inspired to pursue careers in science and science teaching. Both aims appear to me to be wishful thinking.

In summary, my argument is that the new science GCSEs will not only fail to deliver the goal of a less anxious populace, but also, since their content and approach are built on problematic trends within science education, they will hinder our ability to pass on to students a thorough grounding in the sciences and an appreciation of what science has to offer. The relevance agenda, modularisation, a reduced emphasis on practical work, and the sidelining of teachers by re-branding them as 'knowledge intermediaries', are all antithetical to the serious task of developing a deep appreciation of scientific disciplines in a greater number of students.

There is an alternative vision for science education, based on some simple but clear statements of principle:

1   Science education should be made available to all pupils in compulsory education.

2   Science should be taught as separate subjects: physics, chemistry and biology.
    The courses should reflect each subject as an academic discipline in its own right.
3   Pupils should be taught by specialist subject teachers where at all possible. These are the people most likely to inspire and engage those young people in their charge.

4   'Scientific literacy' should not be a compulsory element of science education in schools.

5   Given the continuation of the current allocation of 20 per cent of curriculum time to science, we should aim to cover far more content in all the three sciences, and raise our ambitions of what we can achieve with pupils in the right environment, rather than

creating problems around every aspect of their learning.

6   Science courses are best examined with a single terminal examination.

These principles will lead to an extension of science, which will benefit all pupils in compulsory education by giving them a deeper understanding of science. I believe the education we give our children is a gift that we as a society endow upon them. As such it should reflect the aspirations we hold out for them and for society as a whole.

Instead of foreclosing our aspirations for young people and seeing them as mere consumers of science, we will do the next generation a far greater service by daring to believe that each and every one of them can, as Steven Hawking so eloquently put it, aspire to 'know the mind of God'.

David Perks is head of physics, Graveney School, London

INSPIRATION THROUGH EXPERTISE

Sir Richard Sykes

'Education is the most powerful weapon which you can use to change the world', Nelson Mandela once observed. There are few parents who do not rate a good education as one of their greatest hopes for their children. David Perks' first-rate exposition of the issues surrounding science education in our schools, therefore, may make uncomfortable reading for those reliant upon the state to fulfil this important duty.

The period around A-level and GCSE results in August is traditionally rich with commentators debating the state of education in the UK. This year has been no different except for the disquiet, more noticeable than usual, over the dearth of budding scientists among the post-16 generation.

To revisit the well-worn statistics for a moment: over the past 20 years, the number of young people studying chemistry at A-level has fallen by 37 per cent; those choosing to study physics has dropped by 56 per cent.

This matters because we need science to understand how the world works and to make it work better. From unlocking the secret of DNA to discovering evidence of the universe's first moments, science is telling us about who and where we are. If it had not been for this pricking of scientific curiosity among our distant ancestors, humankind would not have progressed to stone tools, let alone iPods.

It also matters because the world is growing ever smaller and more competitive. The emerging economies of the Far East are placing great priority on science and technology, and institutions such as my own are seeing a rise in the number of international students we admit – well-educated and motivated young people with a commitment to science increasingly lacking in UK applicants. If we do not turn the next generation on to science there is a real risk that the UK will be relegated to second division in the global economy.

So why are UK students so science-averse? I do not believe it is because science is inherently dull – my own experience completely contradicts that notion. There must be something in the way we are communicating science to young people that is doing the damage.

It is true that grasping scientific concepts takes concerted effort. That doesn't mean that pupils automatically become disengaged but it does mean that teaching is vital. In many state schools, unfortunately, pupils are taught by teachers without a degree in science or maths, meaning they are not learning from people with a first-hand knowledge and experience of the subject. In consequence, many pupils are not being turned on to how exciting science can be.

Like most universities, Imperial College is working to tackle this. One scheme we have pioneered is *INSPIRE*, in which post-doctoral researchers, all highly-trained science enthusiasts, mix lab research with training for a PGCE in schools in the London area. This gives the pupils they teach access to someone fresh from cutting-edge research, with the latest theories and technologies at their fingertips.

This initiative runs alongside a range of outreach programmes including peer tutoring, school visits and over 40 summer schools. These are particularly useful as they give us a real insight into what pupils are studying at school. During the summer months, our campus is filled with young people of all ages who come here for a taste of real science. They build robots and create bangs in laboratories, and each year they tell us how different it is from what they do in the classroom.

When I was at school I was able to get involved in real, hands-on science – dissecting sheep eyeballs and putting combustible chemicals together in labs. I was able to discover first-hand how things work, and that was extremely rewarding and exciting. It seems that in many cases this is no longer happening, and as a result young people are failing to engage with science.

Why is it that science teaching in schools has changed its focus since my day? In examining the evidence, David Perks perceptively unpacks the current debate over whether we should be educating the future citizen or the future scientist. I share his concern that emphasis on the former is damaging our development of the latter.

Of course the desire of educationalists to develop a generation with the ability to interact with the science issues of the day is laudable. Simply reciting a string of formulae without any understanding of how they apply to the world around you is useless – the French mathematician Jules Henri Poincare knew that when he said: 'Just as houses are made of stone, so science is made of facts; but a pile of stones is not a house and a collection of facts is not necessarily science.'

However, a science curriculum based on encouraging pupils to debate science in the news is taking a back-to-front approach. Science should inform the news agenda, not the other way around. Before we can engage the public in an informed debate we need the scientists to do the science. And before the future citizen can contribute to the decision-making process they need to have a good grounding in the fundamentals of science and technology, rather than the soundbite science that state school curricula are increasingly moving towards.

Another important but overlooked point raised by David Perks is that these well-meaning attempts to democratise science are actually reinforcing the inequalities in the education system. As the independent sector loses faith in the mainstream integrated science GCSE, many schools are reverting to teaching three separate sciences. This undoubtedly gives their pupils an advantage over those of state schools when it comes to studying sciences at A-level and university.

No one would deny that access to our great centres of learning should depend solely on ability and motivation, not on income or social status. Among the top universities in the UK, including my own, independent schools are disproportionately represented and we are under a great deal of government pressure to broaden our social mix.

However, the post-18 period is far too late a stage to iron out educational inequalities. While universities are energetically involved in a range of schemes to raise aspiration and achievement in state schools, we can only admit students who are qualified for and able to succeed on our demanding courses. To complete a chemistry degree successfully, a student needs a high standard of prior knowledge. Accepting an underqualified candidate who will struggle to keep up and stands a significant chance of failure would be unfair to them, their fellow students and academic staff. Universities are not to blame if pupils are not adequately prepared for the rigours of higher education.

One of the most rewarding aspects of working in a university is seeing the excitement of young people as they make a discovery or solve a problem for themselves. Our outreach programmes allow us to experience the tremendous enthusiasm of school pupils as they try out hands-on experiments and see the tangible results of their work. What I see everyday at Imperial College convinces me that this decline in science is not irreversible. So what do we need to do?

First of all, we must go back to teaching science as three separate disciplines. This enables students to go on to the specialisation required at A-level and university, and promotes a much more in-depth relationship with each subject.

Secondly, we must promote good science teaching in our schools. For science to be interesting, it must be alive and this means real hands-on experience. When pupils visit Imperial College and are able to see what they can do with the knowledge they have accumulated, they are genuinely excited. We need to make this excitement a year-round school-based experience.

An important part of this is valuing teaching as a profession so that it is a genuine career option for graduates who are being courted by industry. This means not only offering meaningful financial incentives but also re-evaluating the way our society views this important role, so that the school teacher is once more a respected figure.

Imperial's *INSPIRE* scheme is one that could be broadened and adapted nationally so that more young scientists are introduced to teaching, and more pupils are exposed to exciting, cutting-edge science. A variation on this could also be developed to allow pupils to spend time with industrialists, to see for themselves how their knowledge can be applied, where a science qualification could take them and how much they could earn.

Finally, amid all the gloomy predictions, it is important to remember what we are doing right. The pool of UK applicants from which Imperial College can choose may be diminishing, but the students we do have possess many skills lacking in previous generations. The most obvious of these is computing – today's students put the rest of us to shame with their IT wizardry. Another example is project management, with students now coming to us with an enhanced ability to plan and oversee their research in a rounded way.

To paraphrase Tracy Koon, Intel's director of corporate affairs: 'Microchips are made from just two things – sand and brains. We have plenty of the former but a diminishing supply of the latter'. It is the job of schools and universities to supply the brains. It is a responsibility we must take seriously, not just for our economic health but for the sake of our young people, who have the brains and want to use them.

Sir Richard Sykes is Rector of Imperial College London

LISTENING TO PUPILS

Michael Reiss

There is much in David Perks' paper with which I find myself in agreement. We need a school curriculum that excites and inspires pupils and results in many of them wanting to study science post-16. Teachers are of paramount importance and we need more excellent, specialist teachers of physics and chemistry (and mathematics too). Practical work is core to science education. We have got ourselves in a mess with regard to how science is assessed at school. There is a real tension between producing a science curriculum that is for future scientists and one that is for all pupils. If we aren't careful, we are heading for a crisis with respect to quality physics teaching in the majority of 11-16 state schools.

At the same time, there are points of difference between us. I am more positive than he about listening to pupils. For one thing, if we don't listen we risk losing even more of them from science once they get to the age when the subject is no longer compulsory. Laboratory experiments, for all that I am in favour of them, are not the be-all-and-end-all of science. If they were, much of astronomy, ecology and the earth sciences would be excluded. We want pupils to have as good an understanding as they can of when scientists should undertake a laboratory experiment, when they should gather data in the field, when they should run a computer simulation, when they should undertake theoretical work and when they should acknowledge that the question cannot yet be answered or isn't scientific. (Think about which of these approaches should be used to see if the speed of light is changing, if aspartame causes cancer, if we are over-fishing cod, if global warming is causing more hurricanes and if Pluto is a planet.)

Here I only have space to concentrate on the core issue: 'What is science education for?' [1]

SUPPLY OF FUTURE SCIENTISTS

A frequent aim of many science courses has been to provide a preparatory education for the small proportion of individuals who will become future scientists (in the commonly understood sense as employed professionals). This aim has been widely and, in my view, validly critiqued on democratic grounds. [2] After all, what of the great majority of school pupils who will not become such scientists?

1   Reiss, M. J. (in press), 'What should be the aim(s) of school science education?' in Corrigan, D., Dillon, J. and Gunstone, R. (eds.), *The Re-emergence of Values in the Science Curriculum*, Sense, Rotterdam

2   For example, by Millar, R. and Osborne, J. (eds.), *Beyond 2000: Science Education for the Future*, Nuffield Foundation, London (1998)

Nevertheless there may be a danger that attempts to craft new science courses so as to make them more relevant to all pupils will result in some of those who would previously have gone on to study science not doing so. It is possible that precisely those features that make certain science courses unpopular to the majority of students (impersonality, objectivity, the absence of value judgements) may make them attractive to those with a particular bent for mainstream professional science.[3]

SCIENTIFIC LITERACY

Generally, scientific literacy is seen as a vehicle to help tomorrow's adults to understand scientific issues.[4] The basic notion is that science education should aim to enhance understanding of key ideas about the nature and practice of science as well as some of the central conclusions reached by science.

Then there is the 'science as culture' argument: that science is as worth studying in itself as are, for example, literature and the arts. Unfortunately, most school science courses don't do a very good job of introducing science as culture. They are short on history and they typically teach little or nothing of the parts of science that the cultural argument would surely deem important, such as evolution, the brain, nanoscience, the origin and end of the universe, the theory of relativity, the uncertainty principle and quantum theory.

INDIVIDUAL BENEFIT

Many science courses hope that, as a result of what is learnt, pupils both now and as adults will be able to benefit from it. At its most straightforward this might be by entering paid employment that draws on what they have learnt in science.

Although, as noted above, most students do not enter such careers, they too may still benefit individually from their school science. For example, in most science courses in countries around the world it has long been accepted that one of the justifications for the inclusion of certain topics is that knowledge and understanding of them can promote human health. Such topics may include infectious diseases, diet, reproduction and contraception and the use of drugs (including smoking and alcohol).

3   Reiss, M. J., 'The importance of affect in science education' in Alsop, S. (ed.), *The Affective Dimensions of Cognition: Studies from Education in the Sciences*, Kluwer, Dordrecht (2005), pp. 17-25

4   Gräber, W. and Bolte, C. (eds.), *Scientific literacy: an international symposium IPN 154*, Institut für die Pädagogik der Naturwissenschaften an der Universität Kiel, Kiel (1997)

Another way in which school science might help individual advancement is by providing what we might term 'science education for consumerism'. This is the hope that school science education might, for example, help us choose the most appropriate technological goods (is it worth my paying x per cent more for a fridge that uses y per cent less power?). This is a sub-set of the more general argument that science education should be for public understanding.[5]

However, in a review of the knowledge actually used by members of the public (i.e. non-scientists) to function effectively in particular settings, Ryder (2001) concluded that the amount of formal scientific knowledge needed was quite limited.[6]

Constructing a science curriculum on the basis of what science members of the public need is likely to result in less emphasis being paid to content knowledge and more to ways of accessing and evaluating scientific knowledge, including procedural knowledge, than is typically provided by school science courses.

DEMOCRACY

Longbottom and Butler have put forward the argument that 'the primary justification for teaching science to all children is that it should make a significant contribution to the advancement of a more truly democratic society'.[7]

The argument that school science education should promote democracy is related to the argument that it should be for citizenship.[8] In both cases there is what we might term a 'weak version' and a 'strong version'. The weak versions consist of learning about what a democracy is and what it is to be a citizen. The strong versions entail using such knowledge in action to bring about change. These strong versions are closely allied to claims that the aim of school science education should be to effect social justice.

SOCIAL JUSTICE

Recent years have seen a growth in the idea that school science education should serve to achieve social justice. For example, Calabrese Barton, who has worked with homeless inner-city children in the USA to develop more appropriate science learning, has shown

5   American Association for the Advancement of Science, *Science for all Americans: Project 2061*, Oxford University Press, New York (1990)

6   Ryder, J., 'Identifying science understanding for functional scientific literacy', *Studies in Science Education*, 36 (2001), pp. 1-44

7   Longbottom, J. E. and Butler, P. H., 'Why teach science? Setting rational goals for science education', *Science Education*, 83 (1999), pp. 473-92

8   Thomas, J., 'Using current controversies in the classroom: opportunities and concerns', *Melbourne Studies in Education*, 41(2) (2000), pp. 133-44

that active participation in science lessons, and real learning about science, take place when children believe that their work can bring about improvements for themselves, their friends and their families.[9] She draws on feminist approaches to show that many of the students with whom she and her colleagues worked, whilst seen in school as poor attainers in science, were actually perfectly capable of high quality science work, provided they were given real choice in the science they worked at.

CRITICALITY

Almost everyone is in favour of critical thinking where 'critical' is taken to mean rigorous, analytical, logical, open-minded and penetrating, and may have elements of reflective scepticism. Critical thinking has blossomed, with courses aimed at all age groups. Hildebrand (2001) has argued in favour of what she terms 'critical activism' in science education.[10] She urges that there should be both participation in science (doing science) and participation in debates about science (challenging science).

Work on critical pedagogy has had a wide influence, but particularly on environmental education which, like health education, sits either within or alongside science education. Huckle, for example, argues that critical education for sustainability is not only focused on a particular construction of sustainability but also based on a critical process of reflection and action in which people are able to participate in the social construction of their environment and sustainability.[11]

The examples in the section above on science for social justice may inspire, but they may also overwhelm or even dishearten. After all, not all science teachers work in ways that allow them to undertake extended projects with their students as reported above. However, it is possible that much classroom-based teaching, over shorter time spans, can contribute to science for criticality. In Reiss (2003) I provide examples in different areas of science for 8-11 year-olds, for 12-14 year-olds and for 15-16 year-olds.[12] Science for criticality still requires students to learn the fundamentals of science and to undertake high quality practical work, but it also involves them grappling with problems to some of which there may be no easy answer.

 For example, when teaching about nuclear power one might want students to undertake

9   Calabrese Barton, A., 'Science education in urban settings: seeking new ways of praxis through critical ethnography', *Journal of Research in Science Teaching*, 38 (2001), pp. 899-917

10   Hildebrand, G. M., 'Con/testing learning models', Conference paper presented at the Annual Meeting of the National Association for Research in Science Teaching, St Louis (2001)

11   Huckle, J., 'Locating environmental education between modern capitalism and postmodern socialism: a reply to Lucie Sauvé', *Canadian Journal of Environmental Education*, 4 (1999), pp. 36-45

12   Reiss, M.J., 'Science education for social justice', in Vincent, C. (ed.), *Social Justice, Education and Identity*, RoutledgeFalmer, London (2003), pp. 153-65

some of the following:

- Research the roles played by such scientists as Henri Becquerel, Ernest Rutherford, Marie Curie and Lise Meitner.
- Plot a map of the distribution of nuclear power stations around the globe and suggest reasons for the results observed.
- Plot graphs of the decrease in radioactivity in vegetation in Cumbria in the years after Chernobyl and compare the results with government predictions.
- Explain how carbon dioxide emissions from electricity-producing stations in France fell by two-thirds in the 1980s.
- Write to both pro- and anti-nuclear power organisations asking them the same specific questions, for example 'How safe is nuclear power?' and 'How important is nuclear power for electricity generation?'
- Examine the medical evidence for and against an increase in the incidence of leukaemia around certain nuclear power stations.
- Design and use a questionnaire to investigate fellow pupils' knowledge of and attitudes towards nuclear power.
- Role-play a cabinet meeting trying to decide whether to extend a country's nuclear power programme or to scrap it.
- Write an imaginary letter from one of the service persons or indigenous people on test islands like Bikini Atoll.

CONCLUSIONS

All curriculum reforms meet resistance. As many (for example, Ogborn, 2002; the Action Research movement) point out, successful change only happens when teachers are fully involved in the changes.[13] Equally, there is increasing acknowledgement that the views of pupils need to be taken into account in the construction of new science courses and pedagogies (for example, Cerini et al., 2003).[14]

At the same time, we have surprisingly little rigorous evidence about what stakeholders other than science educators, science teachers and pupils feel should be the aims of science education. Osborne and Collins (2000) and Reiss (2000) present data on parents' views,[15] and a more recent study that looked at the views of community leaders in Victoria, Australia, found five main purposes expressed for science education: cultural, democratic,

13 Ogborn, J., 'Ownership and transformation: teachers using curriculum innovation', *Physics Education*, 37 (2002), pp. 142-6

14 Cerini, B., Murray, I. and Reiss, M., 'Student Review of the Science Curriculum: Major Findings', Planet Science, London (2003) Available at **http://www.planet-science.com/sciteach/review/Findings.pdf**

15 Osborne, J. and Collins, S., 'Pupils' and Parents' Views of the School Science Curriculum: A study funded by the Wellcome Trust, King's College London, London (2000); and Reiss, M. J., *Understanding Science Lessons: Five Years of Science Teaching*, Open University Press, Buckingham (2000)

economic, personal development, utilitarian.[16]

Finally, although I am of the view that school science education needs more education for social justice and criticality, I have some sympathy with a more conservative analysis:

The central task of a compulsory school science education for all is surely to introduce students to the key features of how scientists understand the material world. It is not to train students to think like scientists, save when they are addressing scientific problems, nor is it primarily to engage them in socio-political issues that have a scientific dimension. Such engagement is better undertaken by (or in conjunction with) others whose training and expertise fits them to handle ethical, moral and political controversy, and might be better accommodated within lessons or activities devoted to citizenship or personal and social education. More fundamentally, such engagement again exposes and challenges the limitations of a subject-based curriculum.[17]

In fact, both for reasons of practicality and because I am suspicious of monolithic arguments, I see a role for a diversity of aims for science education. There are two main reasons for favouring, or at any rate accepting, a number of even incommensurate aims for science. One is that, pragmatically, attempting to insist on just one aim is unlikely to succeed. The second is the possibility that different aims may suit different audiences.

Michael Reiss is professor of science education at the Institute of Education, London and director of education, the Royal Society

16 Symington, D. and Tytler, R., 'Community leaders' views of the purposes of science in the compulsory years of schooling', *International Journal of Science Education*, 26 (2004), pp. 1403-18

17 Jenkins, E., 'Science', in White, J. (ed.), *Rethinking the School Curriculum: Values, Aims and Purposes*, RoutledgeFalmer, London (2004), pp. 165-78

CUT THE CRAP

Simon Singh

Science education has two purposes. First, it should help create a scientifically literate population that is able to engage in debates on how modern research impacts on our daily lives. Second, it should inspire and supply the next generation of scientists, which includes doctors, engineers, meteorologists and anybody else whose career relies on physics, chemistry or biology.

I have no idea whether the first objective is being met. However, I do know that our current science education is dismally failing to meet the second objective.

Every politician responsible for education, science or industry over the past twenty years has allowed science education to decline miserably in terms of its mission to create new scientists. Politicians' relentless neglect has resulted in a shortage of creative, rational, logical thinkers, exactly the sort of people who become inventors, innovators and pioneers. And, without such people, Britain faces a bleak economic future.

Before going any further – what is the evidence that indicates that we are failing to create the next generation of scientists? The most damning fact is that the number of physics A-level students has dropped by half over the last quarter of a century!

That fact alone means that every year there are tens of thousands of students who should be studying physics A-level, but who have dropped the subject because they have not had a half-decent teacher to educate and inspire them. At an individual level, every single one of these lost students is failing to reach their potential. At a national level, we are watching the crumbling of Britain's position at the forefront of science and technology.

This is crap. This is complete crap. This is crap at every possible scale, from nano-crap to galactic crap, from sub-nuclear crap to cosmic crap. I apologise for the repeated use of the word crap, but eight uses of the word crap is roughly equivalent to the word I was forbidden to use.

You might ask me, why am I focusing on physics, as opposed to biology or chemistry? First, we are living in an age when we need physicists more than ever before. It is today's A-level physicists who tomorrow will understand global warming, develop new forms of energy and invent new lucrative technologies. Physicists also make invaluable contributions in unlikely places, ranging from the biotech industry to the stock market. Second, I suspect that the decline in school physics indicates a trend that will hit the other sciences in due course. Chemistry is already suffering similar problems in recruiting students, and biology seems likely to struggle in the years ahead.

So what needs to be done to restore the health of physics education? The challenge for the Secretary of State for Education is to revive school physics back to where it was a quarter of a century ago. This would mean increasing the number of physics A-level entries by 3,000 students each and every year for the next decade. Frankly, I do not care how he, or his successors, reach this target, but in case it is of the slightest interest here are my own thoughts on how to get school physics back on track.

First, is the new science curriculum going to help or hinder school physics? Although I agree with many of the points in David Perks' essay (for example, not enough science practicals, not enough qualified teachers), I do not agree with his full-blooded attack on the new GCSE science curriculum. I think the new style of school science might be very good ... but only for those students who do not intend to pursue science at A-level. As far as I can tell, students who are not inclined towards science are currently bored by the fact-based, theoretical, abstract science. Many of them leave school despising science. Maybe the new context-led GCSE will help transform these frustrated and bored students into ones with a curiosity and interest in the scientific issues that will affect their future.

However, I do agree with David Perks when he says that the new science GCSE offers little hope in terms of creating the next generation of A-level physics students, because it only seems to encourage the study of what might be called 'combined science'.

Currently, the majority of GCSE students study combined science, which means that physics, chemistry and biology are bundled together. Depending on how much is studied, students can receive either one or two GCSEs in combined science. In many schools, combined science is the only form of science that is taught at GCSE.

In contrast, a minority of GCSE students study what are called the separate sciences, i.e.

physics, chemistry and biology being studied separately, thus leading to three distinct GCSEs. It is accepted throughout the education system that the best grounding for studying A-level physics is to complete a GSCE that specifically covers physics, as opposed to one or two combined science GCSEs. Hence, the most obvious improvement to address the shortage of future physicists would be to encourage the availability and teaching of separate science GCSEs (physics, chemistry and biology) for any student who shows enough enthusiasm and aptitude. The majority of students will always opt for combined science GCSEs, but it should be achievable every year to steer several thousand more students towards GCSEs devoted specifically to physics, chemistry and biology.

While encouraging stronger students to do more science by completing three separate science GCSEs (physics, chemistry and biology), I would also encourage average and weaker students do less science by offering combined science only as a single GCSE. Remember, combined science can be worth one or two GCSEs, and I am advocating that the double combined science GCSE option is redundant. To summarise:

1   If students have a strong aptitude for science, then they study three separate science GCSEs (physics, chemistry and biology).

2   If students are average or weaker then they study one combined science GCSE.

3   There would also be some flexibility. For example, a student might choose one combined science GCSE and biology GCSE, or a student might choose biology and chemistry (but not physics) GCSEs if they are interested in preparing for a degree in pharmacy or biochemistry.

By encouraging more bright students to study three separate science GCSEs (physics, chemistry and biology) and by also encouraging the remainder to complete just a single combined science GCSE, there would be a series of significant advantages:

1   There is a drastic shortage of physics and chemistry teachers, but a greater emphasis on separate subject GCSEs will focus their skills. Instead of teaching combined science (and topics outside their knowledge base), teachers can focus on teaching their specialist subject.

2   This will also mean that it will be easier to recruit and retain specialist science teachers, who much prefer teaching their own subject (physics, chemistry or biology) GCSE, rather than the combined science GCSE.

3   The immense stress caused by the shortage of science teachers is slightly relieved by fewer science lessons being taught, because a large number of students currently completing a double combined science GCSE would in future study for a single combined science GCSE.

4   If more students study separate science GCSEs, then they will be better prepared for A-levels, so the A-level can be beefed up back to its earlier levels of detailed study.

Obviously it is not ideal for a large number of average students to drop from double to single combined science GCSE, as it means that more students are studying less science. However, we do not live in an ideal world.

If I had my way, each and every student would be personally tutored by a holographic reincarnation of Richard Feynman, but it is not going to happen. Instead, given the constraints of a limited timetable, limited numbers of teachers, and limited enthusiasm from some students, then it makes sense to focus resources where they will have the most impact. Also, the students who spend less time on science will be able to spend more time studying languages, arts or whatever else inspires them.

On its own, a greater emphasis on separate science GCSEs will not be enough to save science in schools, because there exists a severe shortage of specialist physics and chemistry teachers. Unless this problem is properly addressed, then it will sabotage any other investment aimed at improving science education. You will hear others say that the uptake in science depends on making science sexy, more classroom experiments, putting science in context and emphasising the career options – but these are all red herrings, inasmuch as you get them for free with a decent teacher at the front of the class. Hence, the Department for Education and Skills needs to redouble its efforts to recruit new teachers, and then redouble its efforts again in order to achieve the number of A-level physics students we had in the early 1980s.

The reason that I am making such a fuss about the crisis in science education is that everything I have ever achieved in my career has been as a result of my education in physics. I was enthralled by physics because I had a great teacher and a challenging curriculum in the shape of physics O-level. My parents left India and came to the UK so that I could receive this sort of excellent education, but the tables are gradually turning. While Indian science education has improved significantly over the last decade, British science education is going down the drain.

The good news is that the UK government is making the right sort of noises about the importance of recruiting more specialist science teachers and making separate science GCSEs more available. The bad news is that nobody in government is actually going to do anything.

For the past twenty-five years ministers have whined about the decline in science education, but nobody has cared enough to get off his or her backside and halt this decline. And, unfortunately, there is no reason to believe that the current bunch of ministers is going to behave any differently from their feckless predecessors.

Simon Singh is a science writer and broadcaster

THE PATRONISING INDIGNITY OF TWENTY FIRST CENTURY SCIENCE

Baroness Mary Warnock

I have long been appalled by my own scientific illiteracy. As far as physics goes, I have hardly advanced beyond Lucretius. In chemistry, because I had a sister who reluctantly read chemistry at Oxford and taught me a little during vacations in order to aid her own learning, I once knew a bit more, but have forgotten it all. Such biology as I know has been picked up from admirable and willing teachers on my embryology committee in the 1980s.[1]

I was therefore at first pleased by the idea that the pilot Twenty First Century Science syllabus might work, to provide for GCSE students a basic understanding of the disciplines of science and of the nature of things that I never had. However, it soon became clear that the emphasis in this syllabus is less on basic understanding than on 'relevance': in other words, on controversial issues. It is less science than morals and politics.

Moreover, I had not realised that the new GCSE in scientific literacy is to be compulsory, for future scientists and non-scientists alike. In my view, this is a recipe for disaster; and as I read David Perks' essay I was totally convinced and greatly alarmed.

His most striking observations came in the section 'The death of the experimental method?' There Perks argues that because controversial issues are often, broadly speaking, medical, 'the controlled laboratory experiment – the backbone of modern scientific enquiry – is being replaced by the field study'. This has wide-ranging consequences. The first is that students do not have the chance to see how scientific laws are established by controlled experiment. This means that they begin to regard science not as a strict discipline seeking to establish laws, but, like sociology, as a matter of using observation (field study) to suggest interpretations that are open to dispute.

Other observations, other conclusions. Such relativism fits all too readily into the pattern of postmodern chaos that passes for deep thought not only among students, but, alas, among teachers who are 'philosophically' inclined. All points of view are equally valid. There is no place here for a young scientist's growing passion to find the truth, how things actually are, because there is no one truth, only your truth and mine. So science itself falls into disrepute.

1 The Committee on Human Fertilisation and Embryology, chaired by Mary Warnock, published its landmark report into the social, ethical and legal implications of recent and potential developments in the field of human assisted reproduction in 1984.

Moreover what counts as an Issue to be debated in class is largely, as David Perks points out, dictated by the press. The new GCSE class could take as its textbook a series of cuttings from, say, the *Daily Mail* on one hand and the *Guardian* on the other. Far too much teaching at school has already degenerated into this kind of debate (think, for example, of religious education or philosophy), more suitable for the pub than the school-room. The knowledge base of such debates must necessarily be not only second- or third-hand but essentially superficial.

We know that fewer and fewer students take physics at A-level (especially in the maintained schools); and this means that fewer read physics (or chemistry) at university. There is therefore a severe shortage of qualified specialist school teachers. But perhaps this will no longer matter. If GCSE science is a matter of 'argumentative discourse' and the consideration of 'plural alternatives' (see the quotations from Jonathan Osborne) there is no need for specialists. Anyone who can chair a discussion group will do. Dumbing down and postmodern relativism go hand in hand.

So what is to be done? Is it already too late to rescue real science except in the independent schools? It seems to be going the way of Latin and Greek. But at least the universities have found ways for students to begin those subjects when they come up. They cannot be expected to do the same in the sciences.

The present policy has two incompatible aims: to give all pupils some understanding of the subject matter of the sciences, and to so fire the imagination of a substantial minority of them that they want to pursue their interest into the sixth form and beyond. Neither of these aims can be achieved by the Twenty First Century Science GCSE.

I believe that the first of these aims could be achieved best by a compulsory (though flexible) four-year course starting at the age of 11 that would fit on to primary school science; it would consist of an introduction to all the sciences, taught by specialists who understood the scientific method, and were enthusiastic about the discipline of laboratory work. Something of the history of scientific advances and conceptual changes (the history and philosophy of science) would be taught at this stage; and non-school science subjects, such as geology, botany, palaeontology and astronomy, would be introduced, perhaps sometimes by visitors, brought in from outside school to fill the gaps in the regular teachers' knowledge or enthusiasm. And full use could be made of field trips, and trips to science museums and telescopes.

The essential target of this part of the curriculum would be the imagination and curiosity of the pupils, to instil in them a respect for the whole enterprise of science and a longing to know more. The politics of the applications of science should be kept as far away as possible. The idea that only such 'topical' controversies can interest children is preposterous, literally. It is to put the cart before the horse. But this part of scientific education needs to come early: what the primary curriculum has started, the secondary should reinforce.

With this background, common to all pupils, those who wanted to find out more could then take three separate subjects at GCSE, going to local colleges or independent schools for their lessons as long as the shortage of specialist teachers persisted. Those whose curiosity had led them to this course would not find the work involved excessively dry or boring. They would understand the enterprise on which they were engaged. I an convinced that this is the way to ensure that pupils are not 'turned off' science.

Ideally (and if only the Tomlinson recommendations had been properly accepted [2]), some pupils would substitute vocational for theoretical subjects at the age of fourteen. But they would still benefit from the kind of science teaching they had had in their first years at secondary school; and they might be spared the patronising indignity of the Twenty First Century Science GCSE altogether. Those non-scientists who had to take it would also have benefited from their earlier teaching, and, knowing something of the history of scientific advances, might be more inclined to recognise that scientific laws are not matters of mere opinion, and therefore to put trust in properly conducted research.

2   A government-commissioned review of the curriculum for 14 to 19-year-olds, led by the former Ofsted chief Mike Tomlinson, in 2004 proposed replacing GCSEs, A-levels and vocational qualifications with a new single diploma over a 10-year period of reform.

TWENTY FIRST CENTURY SCIENCE: THE CASE FOR CHANGE

Andrew Hunt

There are two equally important aims for science education:

- to develop the 'scientific literacy' of all students, and
- to provide the foundation for more advanced study in science.

Unfortunately, David Perks misrepresents the Twenty First Century Science programme by suggesting that its main aim is to develop scientific literacy. This is not the case. The Twenty First Century Science team is strongly committed to both aims. The project is exploring the hypothesis that these aims are better achieved by separate courses running in parallel, rather than by courses that try to achieve both aims within a single programme.

SCIENTIFIC LITERACY

Perks is not in favour of 'scientific literacy' as an aim of science education, and yet he points to the sales of popular science books like Bill Bryson's *A Short History of Nearly Everything* as an indicator that science is of great interest to young people. The irony is that Bill Bryson was profoundly bored by conventional science education. As Bryson makes clear in the introduction to his book, his first school science textbook excited his interest with a diagram of the inside of the Earth but then failed him by not answering 'any of the questions that the illustration stirred up in a normally enquiring mind'.

Bill Bryson wanted answers to the question 'How do they know that?' He was frustrated to find that teachers and textbook writers failed to help with this type of question. *A Short History of Nearly Everything* is an account of his personal quest, as an adult, to discover not just what scientists know but also how they know it. It goes on to explore the questions that science at the frontiers is trying to answer, and then how the answers might be found. His book is a compelling exemplification of what it means to be scientifically literate, as envisaged by the Twenty First Century Science team.

Perks does not seem to think that asking questions about 'How we know' should be given prominence in science education. His educational approach is summed up by the statement that 'teenagers have a simple approach to education: they want to know what the answer is'. So, in his view, the job of teachers is simply to supply students 'with the building blocks of knowledge, which act as a foundation for their understanding'.

RELEVANCE

In one part of his paper, Perks is surprised that anyone should take seriously the interests of learners – beyond responding to their demand for 'the answers'. Unfortunately he confuses child-centredness, context-led approaches and relevance. He broadly treats them as parts of a syndrome arising from a diseased approach to science education.

In a child-centred approach, it is young people who decide what they would like to learn about. The new GCSEs are in no way child-centred. In developing their scientific literacy, students have to learn a substantial number of major scientific theories selected by the course designers; they also have to grasp an intellectually challenging and coherent set of ideas that explain how scientists gather valid data, develop explanations and apply what they have learnt.

Twenty First Century Science offers an approach to teaching about 'How science works' developed by Robin Millar, Jonathan Osborne and others. The AQA specifications offer a related but rather different approach, which has been developed by Richard Gott. The selection of content is based on research and not on what young people say they want.

Both these approaches to 'How science works' are a valuable part of the education for all, including those who will go on to study science further. What they learn in this strand of their GCSE science will underpin more advanced approaches to valid methods of investigation and rigorous approaches to interpreting evidence. This lays stress on 'how we know' and how we find out about what we don't yet know: matters of passionate concern to professional scientists.

Twenty First Century Science unashamedly seeks to 'engage students with concepts and ideas beyond their immediate frame of reference', but in doing so it tries to show teachers how these concepts and ideas can have significance for young people. Making learning meaningful is essential – it does not imply dumbing down.

In its various GCSE programmes, Twenty First Century Science uses a variety of approaches. Sometimes the approach is context-led, sometimes concept-led, and sometimes the way in is through applied and work-related topics

COHERENCE

Perks also worries about approaches to science that break the subject into 'bite-sized chunks'. His arguments against the excessive modularisation of assessment are well made. The Twenty First Century Science team certainly shares this concern: hence an approach to teaching the theory that stresses the coherence of ideas and explanations, backed up by an assessment model which includes an end-of-course test requiring students to show that they can make connections between their learning in differing parts of the courses.
Biology, chemistry and physics

David Perks is wrong in saying that maintained schools have to choose between the demanding option of three separate sciences or and the more 'relevant' suite of Twenty First Century Science courses. The Twenty First Science programme provides separate science GCSE courses in biology, chemistry and physics.

Even within the Science and Additional Science GCSEs, the separate sciences are clearly delineated with distinct biology, chemistry and physics modules. The GCSE Additional Science course, in particular, is designed to highlight differences in the methods of inquiry and the key concepts in the different sciences.

Choices in science education should not be made in isolation from the rest of the curriculum. There is an 'opportunity cost' for students if they take three subjects-worth of science at the expense of other valuable areas of learning such as languages, humanities and creative arts. Arguably the bigger barrier to progression in the physical science for many young people is not their knowledge and understanding of science, but their confidence and competence in mathematics.

TEACHING AND LEARNING

David Perks is very right to highlight the importance of having well-qualified and expert teachers, but he makes unwarranted assertions about present priorities for professional development. One of the former co-directors of the Twenty First Century Science Project now directs the National Science Learning Centre. The Wellcome Trust funded this centre because of the need for subject-specific professional development.

The limits of 'specialist subject knowledge' were brought home to me during my induction into teaching at Manchester Grammar School in 1964. In front of a class, Sol Clynes (of O-level chemistry textbook fame) used just a few chemicals and test tubes to show me that, despite a Cambridge degree in Natural Sciences, I had a lot to learn about 'the best ways of teaching specific science content and concepts to particular groups of students'. Any reflective teacher knows that a good science degree is not enough. Good teachers constantly need to learn fresh skills and ideas.

One of the things that makes science teaching intellectually stimulating is the quest for new and better ways to teach. As science advances, it is a continuing challenge for teachers to develop the language, symbols and experiences that can make new areas of knowledge meaningful to younger learners.

David Perks is also wrong to say that those involved in teacher training are not interested in helping teachers with exciting laboratory experiments and demonstrations. For example, the Nuffield Curriculum Centre, one of the lead organisations in Twenty First Century Science, is working with the Institute of Physics and Royal Society of Chemistry to develop websites with full details about hundreds of exciting laboratory experiments and demonstrations, which remain of central importance in science education (see http://www.practicalphysics.org). At the same time they are putting on related courses for teachers in the Science Learning Centres.

Perks suggests that the critics of 'traditional' science teaching have adopted a shallow pastiche of the truth that only serves to flatter the new thinking about science education. Unfortunately he uses similar tactics in his dismissal of the work of Professor Jonathan Osborne. Were he to watch some of the video clips in the IDEAS pack, for example, he would see that the teachers play a central role, but use methods to develop critical thinking skills that encourage learners to engage with the sorts of questions that excite Bill Bryson – questions related not to 'issues' but to key science concepts.

PRACTICAL WORK

Perks implies that there is less practical work in the new GCSEs. This is certainly not the case in Twenty First Century Science. The purposes of practical work in each of the courses in the programme are different. The extent and diversity of practical work are matched to the aims of each course. Overall there is no less practical work for those doing two or three science GCSEs than in the double-award courses. Even the minority doing just the single, scientific literacy course will experience a good range of practical work.

Furthermore, practical work becomes more meaningful and purposeful as young people develop what Richard Gott calls 'procedural understanding' alongside their 'conceptual understanding'.

David Perks asserts that the level of complexity involved in appreciating the experimental method in the new GCSEs is far below that acknowledged previously at Key Stage 4. This is simply not the case for the Twenty First Century Science programme which, unlike some other new GCSEs, has retained the requirement for a 'whole investigation' by students taking Additional Science, while changing the assessment criteria for investigations to legitimise a much wider a range of practical laboratory and field inquiries than has been permitted by the national curriculum to date.

Perks makes the puzzling statement that 'the controlled laboratory experiment – the backbone of modern scientific enquiry – is being replaced by the field study'. A little later he states that the approach based on controlled laboratory experiments is the source of science's greatest discoveries. This is not the conclusion which a reader of Bill Bryson's book would come to after reading about scientific investigations of the solar system and the universe, of rocks and fossils and the evolution of life on earth.

FOR OR AGAINST IDEAS?

Perks seems to think that the nature and content of science education is self-evident and that all we have to do is to teach biology, chemistry and physics and all will be well. But the designers of any GCSE course have to make choices. Sometimes these choices are based on a coherent rationale informed by experience and research. Sometimes they are based more on 'gut feeling'.

The choices made change with time. The Nuffield projects of the 1960s were a response by teachers in independent and grammar schools, inspired by a profound dissatisfaction with the science curriculum of the 1950s. The developments in the 1970s and 1980s arose as teachers rose to the challenge of providing a worthwhile science education to everyone in school, and not just to a select minority in grammar schools. The ambition to teach 'science for all' called for much fresh thinking, and started an adventure that many of us have enjoyed ever since.

In the 1990s, the National Curriculum, with its programme of testing backed up by inspection and league tables, led to a compliance culture which stifled innovation and fresh thinking in schools. Now, in the twenty-first century, the regulators have drawn back and allowed greater flexibility. Teachers can again make choices about the type of science education they offer to the young people in their schools.

This is an exciting time to be debating ideas – and finding effective ways to implement them in practice. With Bill Bryson we should be helping young people 'to marvel at – enjoy even – the wonder and accomplishments of science'.

Andrew Hunt is director of the Nuffield Curriculum Centre and co-director of the Twenty First Century Science project

FOR SCIENTIFIC LITERACY <u>AND</u> PRACTICAL SCIENCE

Dr Eliot Forster

In his essay 'What is science education for?' David Perks expresses his concerns about the future of science education in the UK. He conveys what seems to be an increasingly widely-held viewpoint: that the erosion of practical science in schools, exemplified by the new GCSE curriculum, is misguided and driven by a 'desire to empower students as future citizens and consumers of science *not* producers of it'. His ultimate concern is that this 'can only result in a negative downward pressure on the uptake of the physical sciences at both A-level and undergraduate level for pupils from state schools'.

The declining number of students pursuing science beyond GCSE level is undoubtedly a concern – personally and professionally in my case. But before we lay the blame for this at the feet of schools and government, we must consider a significant contributory factor that is cultural and lies beyond the influence of any teacher or policy-maker.

The Rose Project[1] examined young people's attitudes to science education, and revealed that students from developed countries have significantly more negative views of science than students in developing countries. This is something I have observed first-hand on trips to countries such as India, China and Singapore, where there is a tangible enthusiasm for science and a growing pool of world-class scientific talent. In these countries, there is a real hunger for scientific endeavour, largely fuelled by the desire for economic growth and improved public health.

In the UK, many of us have forgotten (and some will never have understood) how instrumental science was in delivering the quality of life we enjoy today. The benefits of science are reaped without a thought as to how they have been made possible.

As a result, I believe our appetite for science has waned. The public standing of science has diminished and fewer children are studying it. This is a trend we need to address, and I share Perks' view that one of the best ways to do this is to provide children with the chance to do practical science – to conduct experiments. However, we must also remember that science education has to cater for all needs and abilities, and that it is a minority of children who are capable enough and have the desire to make careers out of science.

1   Young People and Science:
    Attitudes, Values and Priorities
    **http://www.ils.uio.no/english/
    rose/network/countries/
    norway/eng/nor-sjoberg-
    eu2005.pdf**

Bearing this in mind, I think improving the 'scientific literacy' of the next generation is a worthwhile aim of science education – and GCSE level is where it needs to be done. What is vital is that it is not done at the expense of practical science, and so denies the pupils who are bright and curious about science the opportunity to experiment and learn important scientific principles. These are the pupils most likely to become tomorrow's inventors, and in doing so conduct research that delivers social benefit for individuals and economic benefit for the nation.

Having observed public debate of science and its bearing on policy decisions, I think greater scientific literacy among the general population could actually benefit science and scientists. I often react to debate around medical and health issues with a mixture of interest, bemusement and frustration.

For example, in the media many medicines are portrayed as either 'magic bullets' or 'toxic killers'. Few are either, but black and white, not shades of grey, sells newspapers. In reality, most drugs sit somewhere between these two descriptors – all medicines have risks as well as benefits associated with them. Surprisingly few patients understand this, and many lack the level of scientific knowledge necessary to cut through the headlines and accurately assess the degree of risk a medicine might present. Nor do they have the knowledge they need to appreciate this must be set against the degree of risk their disease presents should they opt not to take a medicine.

A more scientifically literate population would be able to make more rational, evidence-led decisions on a host of scientific issues, from the potential of GM crops to address food shortages, to whether mobile phones are harmful to health, to why animal research is important and necessary. These issues have an impact on us as individuals and also upon the society in which we live, which is why I believe science education should seek to improve children's scientific literacy.

But it should also be encouraged for another reason. By drawing pupils' attention to current, real world issues – what they see on their TVs at home – it can enthuse children by giving science context and relevance and opening their eyes to the applications of science. I was reminded of this by the findings of a recent Pfizer-sponsored study conducted by *spiked*.[2] When renowned scientists were asked what inspired them to pursue

2   What Inspired You?
    http://www.spiked-
    online.com/index.php?/
    inspired/index/

a career in science, three key influences emerged: the presence of a good teacher; the ability to conduct experiments; and real world events that made them wonder how and why (the space race being an example that seems to have inspired many scientists of a certain generation).

I agree with Perks' view that the most effective way to make children curious about science is to let them conduct experiments. Looking back, my passion for chemistry at school was ignited by exactly this, and it concerns me today that my son seems to do far fewer experiments in his science classes than I ever did. Experiments also teach children the importance of rigour and the scientific method: hypothesis, experiment, data, conclusion.

This is a process all scientists must understand. To find a new drug, medicinal chemists and biologists test and re-test their ideas by conducting experiments, creating data and then drawing conclusions. The journey from hypothesis to understanding is impossible to complete without experiments. This applies to all strands of science and defines what R&D is all about. The fewer people understand it, the greater the challenge becomes – both in terms of science-based industries being able to recruit the talent they need, and the broader population having a sufficiently robust understanding of science for public debate to be informed and appropriate conclusions about new technologies reached.

This issue is of particular concern at a time when industry is repeatedly warning about the challenges posed to the future competitiveness of the UK by the high quality of scientific talent now available overseas, in locations such as India, China, Singapore and Eastern Europe. There is now considerable scientific talent in these countries, and they are ready to compete hard for investment from R&D-based companies. If the UK is to maintain its competitive advantage as a location for pharmaceutical R&D, it needs to take action to ensure that its schools and universities continue to produce science graduates of the highest calibre. A key element of this will be improving science education in schools, not to mention in higher education.

There is one final factor that must not be ignored. No matter what the content of the science curriculum, all pupils will leave school with a better grasp of science if they have been taught by a specialist science teacher with a passion for the subject. The *spiked* survey revealed that a good teacher was the most common source of inspiration for those who have made successful careers out of science. This is true for me too, which is why I find the number of science lessons in state schools being taught by non-specialists so alarming. To address this, we need to keep more children in the science education pipeline for longer, which means giving them more opportunity to experiment.

In summary, I think few people would disagree that there are challenges to be overcome in UK science education. In answering the question 'what is science education for?', Perks expresses a strong belief that its primary role must be the production of scientists. I agree this is an essential function it must perform, but it must also, particularly at school level, have the broader aim of improving the scientific literacy of the pupils with less ability or interest in science.

We need bright young scientists to become tomorrow's inventors and teachers and maintain the UK's competitive edge in a global economy, but tackling the underlying issue of public apathy and mistrust of science requires a higher degree of scientific literacy among a much larger proportion of the UK population. Achieving both of these aims requires policy-makers to avoid treading the path of least resistance by giving practical science sufficient time on the curriculum and ensuring that the importance of this issue is reflected in its funding.

Dr Eliot Forster is Vice President of Development, EU and Asia,
Pfizer Global Research & Development

MAKING SCIENCE COOL

Dr Brian Iddon MP

David Perks' essay has provided us with an excellent platform for debate. He argues that the physical sciences should be taught separately and by specialist teachers in those subjects, and completely rejects the concept of 'scientific literacy'. But surely, there must be room for both in our science courses?

It might be that those who set the science curriculum have got it wrong for the moment, but that is not a good reason for rejecting the idea that our young people are seeking to understand the relevance of what they learn and to debate the current issues in science. In his analysis Perks misses some important points: for example, the influence of the media, and the state of our school laboratories.

I am a member of the House of Commons Science and Technology Select Committee, which published *Science Education from 14 to 19* in 2002. Like our captains of industry and those who run physical science courses in our universities, we are concerned about the closures of university science and engineering departments and the declining numbers of schoolchildren studying physical sciences.

The Committee holds a regular 'Question Time' with Lord Sainsbury, Minister for Science and Innovation, at the Department of Trade and Industry, and on successive occasions we have raised this matter with him. His response is always that the number of young people studying science, especially in our universities, is not going down: at the very least it has remained static and has probably increased, depending on how we define science.

There are just more choices available today. The growth in computer science during my life-time has been astonishing, and this has attracted large numbers of young people into university courses. And many of these new branches of science owe their popularity to the media.

The media, especially television with its multitude of channels, influence all our lives today, and the internet is playing an increasing role. Forensic science, for example, has been glamorised by TV. The result has been a clamour for forensic science courses in our universities. Space is another sexy subject and, as a consequence of its coverage on TV, courses in astronomy have blossomed. In addition, of course, the coverage of health topics by the media has kept the number of young people knocking on the doors of our medical schools high. The same has been true of veterinary science (again, witness the coverage of animal issues on TV), and similarly any course with the word 'environment' in its title.

On the other hand, portrayals in the media may also have a negative effect. Perhaps many of our young people have been 'turned off' by chemistry because the media have painted chemists as polluters of the world rather than as people who make useful things, including medicines that treat killer diseases such as AIDS/HIV. How many times have I been told by young people that they don't like the horrible smells of chemicals – a negative image? But perfumes and air fresheners are chemicals too – a positive image.

Since media influences can therefore act either way, we should never underestimate the power of the media when it comes to influencing the minds of young people. TV is probably more powerful than the careers adviser when it comes to choosing a career. I am not impressed by the careers advice on offer to many of our schoolchildren.

Much of the problem with science as a career comes down to image. The plain fact is that chemistry, physics and mathematics are not regarded as 'cool' subjects to study by our young people. Who wants to be a 'boffin', looking slightly mad and wearing a white coat and those horrible safety glasses? In addition, these are perceived as hard subjects to study.

What does your school laboratory look like? Does it have efficient and modern fume cupboards, and enough of them? Are the benches from the Victorian era, or are they made of materials that can be found in any modern industrial laboratory? By comparison, what does your language laboratory look like?

There is no doubt that we need to continue to invest in our school laboratories. This government has made a start, but the pace is too slow. The 'Building Schools for the Future' programme is an excellent opportunity to build laboratories for the future. The aim is to rebuild or refurbish every secondary school that is in need of renewal. In the next financial year £6 billion is available, increasing to £8 billion by 2010-11.

But it's not just about the appearance and functionality of school science laboratories. As

Perks points out, it is about getting the right staff in place. That means an adequate supply of well-qualified laboratory technicians, as well as specialist teachers. Is it any wonder that teachers shun practical work when they are expected to set up most of the experiments?

In my teaching career I have visited a lot of schools and found a lot of teachers with a lot of excuses for not doing this or that experiment. The number of myths that abound about what is or is not possible in a school laboratory never ceases to amaze me. Yes, it's the litigious society – headteachers are afraid of their school being sued by a parent. That would give the school a bad name, wouldn't it?

Now, I don't pretend that this is an easy matter to confront, but confront it we must. Yes, there are occasional accidents in school laboratories but, with excellent supervision from a teacher who has properly assessed the risks and dealt with them, they can be minimised, if not eliminated. A pupil is at equal risk of having an accident travelling to and from school to having one inside school.

Practical work is attractive to pupils. They like the excitement of handling potentially dangerous materials, and are enthralled by the colour changes and the occasional controlled bang. There are some beautiful experiments, easy and cheap to perform, such as the Tyndall or 'sunset' experiment. A teacher who plays down the significance of practical work risks losing his or her audience. But sadly, teachers often play down the importance of practical work because of syllabus and assessment pressures.

I disagree with Perks on the question of reform of the science curriculum. Some key messages came loud and clear to us when we took evidence for our report *Science Education from 14 to 19*. One of them, also flagged up by Perks, is the damage that 'modular learning' has done – learn it today, forget it tomorrow. To become a good scientist or engineer, the learning process has to bc linear.

Pupils told our committee that they got fed up with learning about the same aspect of science over and over again – photosynthesis, for example, in primary school, and photosynthesis in secondary school. The trouble seems to be that different interpretations of the same subject are given by different teachers at different levels of the learning process, which pupils find not only confusing but a 'turn-off'.

And relevance is a problem. Pupils told us many times that they could not see why they were expected to learn some facts because they could not see the relevance of them. Now, that is probably because the teachers hadn't explained the relevance.

Take the Haber process, which featured in my discussions with pupils. Why do they need to have an extensive knowledge of such an industrial process? Well, it is about nitrogen fixation, and some plants do that too, but not to provide the quantities of nitrates in the soil that are necessary for modern agriculture without crop rotation. What about increases in population, the 'green revolution' and feeding the starving millions in the world? How do we avoid nitrates causing problems in water courses when leached from the soil? Why not have a debate at school? Teachers have to explain the relevance of what they are teaching.

The better schools engage themselves in a number of events and projects that support their science teaching, such as outside lectures, the SEAS (Science and Engineering Ambassadors in Schools) programme, visits to museums, many of which provide 'hands-on' displays and educational programmes, and engagement with the newer forms of teaching science, such as the City Learning Centres.

In Bolton, we have launched the first junior incubator, Bolton Technical Innovation Centre Ltd (TIC), a £2.5 million building equipped with £500,000 of state-of-the-art equipment. The aim is to give all 9-19 year-old children an out-of-mind, out-of-school experience, with a view to allowing the 'turned-on' to manufacture their inventions. The hope is that, eventually, one of the streams of income will arise from new intellectual property rights and the consequent royalties arising from the sale of inventions to local and regional companies.

Bolton TIC is the equivalent of a music centre for STEM (Science, Technology, Engineering and Mathematics) subjects. Just as a music centre brings together all those interested in music to perform at a higher level than they can in an individual school, Bolton TIC does the same for budding scientists and engineers. This project stands outside the Local Education Authority, but is strongly supported by it, and local and regional industry and commerce are welcome to use the building, and do.

We have an artist in residence, who uses our equipment, CAD (Computer Assisted Design) programmes, and the three-dimensional colour printer, for example, to assist in the design of his sculptures. In return, he passes on his knowledge to visiting children, thus bridging the perceived gap between the arts and science.

The local astronomical and aero-modelling societies are given free access to the building, providing they also pass on their skills to the children. Science clubs are under way, and the plan is to invite famous scientists to make presentations at the TIC, which is open at the weekends, in the evenings and throughout the school holidays. This is a 'can do' adventure.

I end by stating the obvious. The best teachers have a love of their subject and can convey their overwhelming enthusiasm to their pupils. They are actors in a theatre. To perform well, they need charisma and should exude the confidence that they are in control of their performance. Behind the scenes, however, they will need the back-up of support staff (including their headteacher) who understand the business.

Dr Brian Iddon is Member of Parliament for Bolton South East

EDUCATION SHOULDN'T BE FUN

Harriet Teare

'There seemed to be a mystifying universal conspiracy among textbook authors to make certain that material they dealt with never strayed too near the realm of mildly interesting ... So I grew up convinced that science was supremely dull, but suspecting that it needn't be.'

Bill Bryson, *A Short History of Nearly Everything*, Black Swan (2004)

In recent years, as I have become more aware of the important issues concerning our society, it has become increasingly clear that in most cases science plays a pivotal role. From organic produce to the MMR vaccine to the use of mobile phones, where there is technology and progress there is science, and where there is scientific research there is controversy and debate.

One of the fundamental problems we are faced with today is that the majority of people don't necessarily understand enough about scientific research to be able to make an educated choice as to whether they agree or not with the work being carried out. This is a fundamental short-fall, and undoubtedly needs to be addressed: but will introducing scientific literacy as a compulsory subject, in the place of real science, really help? Has the government taken the need to 'educate' people a little too literally? Is the classroom the correct debating chamber to raise these complicated questions?

As a research scientist, currently working on my chemistry DPhil, the dispute surrounding science education is a particularly relevant one. Having only recently gone through the system myself, I am all too aware of the difficulties I had to overcome to reach chemistry research, and that was when the curriculum actually included science. I do not see how these newest 'improvements' to the syllabus are going to help, and I am positive that if I had been unfortunate enough to be subject to compulsory scientific literacy I would now be a lawyer.

Without a shadow of a doubt, the content of my science curriculum bore little relevance to my keen interest in the subject. My interest was fuelled by a collection of passionate and enthusiastic teachers who believed in their subject and desperately wanted to share their interest with us: an impressionable group of teenagers hungry for stimulation and information. And it is such teachers that really hold the key to improving scientific learning.

Many of the changes proposed by the government supposedly favour the majority – an unfortunate bunch of individuals who will never understand it all, so why bother? They won't get it, it's too hard, so teach them something less complicated and (supposedly) more relevant and then everyone's happy: even if the entire point in education – to encourage understanding and further people's grasp on a subject – has been missed. Denying teenagers the opportunity even to try to understand goes against everything schooling should stand for, and makes a mockery of equal opportunities. It isn't supposed to be easy, it isn't supposed to be fun. Since when did a subject in the curriculum change because of concerns that some students found it irrelevant?

I am not belittling the need for scientific literacy to be improved. But in the same way that not everyone is going to understand Newton's laws of physics, they are not all going to understand the subtleties in molecular biology enough to contribute to the proposed scientific debates. As a chemical biologist, I would be extremely nervous entering into a debate on GM foods or stem cell research – because despite having spent five years at university studying science, I am not trained to do so. Yet the plan is to allow 14-year-olds, stripped of all science training, to be let loose on these issues, and forced to come to a suitable decision and clear opinion in order to satisfy an exam board.

This proposed curriculum lends no sympathy to the students who develop at a later stage, who at the age of 14 aren't equipped to decide whether a career in science is for them, who require the GCSE course to stretch them and help them explore the subject. Shutting doors and restricting the opportunities to learn at such an early stage can only have an adverse effect on the recruitment of the future scientists for which the government is supposedly so desperate.

And even if, during the scientific literacy GCSE, a student has enough foresight to appreciate her interest in science, on reaching A-level she will be horrified to realise that she is ill-equipped and under-trained to forward her learning at a suitable pace. By the time she starts her science degree, she will be too far behind to enjoy the experience, and her thirst for insight and information will be buried under the desperate struggle to keep her head above water long enough to sustain a pass. This is hardly the making of our next Nobel Prize winner.

The benefit of a broad education bridging a number of different subjects is lost, if children as young as 14 need to have already decided their future career. There is no opportunity for indecision, creativity or simple curiosity. Doing a subject and discovering that you hate it or are abominable at it is surely just as important as discovering an interest or an unexpected talent. Finding something boring, and knowing how it feels to be challenged and to struggle, is as significant in education as being riveted and successful, especially as this is a better reflection on real life.

Without such obstacles and variety, school would be even more boring and students even less motivated, and what would the government propose then? Shorter school days? More computer games, or DVD-watching opportunities? How much further are these young people going to be patronised and short-changed?

In arguing that students should be learning about subjects relevant to their everyday lives, like health and medicine, it seems to me that the entire point is being missed. The production of new pharmaceuticals and the creation of new ways to keep healthy are inextricably linked to chemistry, biology, physics: the very subjects thought too archaic and specialised to interest GCSE students any more. And in order to understand the issues surrounding scientific arguments, is it not fundamentally important to understand where the research has come from in the first place? To appreciate that, when carrying out an experiment, there needs to be a control and a limit to the number of variables changed, and so on?

Without having specifically carried out their own experiments, however rudimentary and seemingly irrelevant, students will not be able to appreciate fully how complicated the science really is. It is the experimental process that is perhaps most important, and it is this element of science that is being overlooked.

The issue that needs to be addressed in science education is not simply the actual science being taught. It is how this information is conveyed to students in an interesting and engaging manner, that allows them to realise how exciting science – and by this I mean the core fundamental principles, the laws of physics, the uncertainty principle, the periodic table – can be, and how they themselves can contribute to the process, or simply appreciate that the process exists. It is the recruitment of teachers who believe in what they are teaching that needs to be addressed and improved upon, not the theory of relativity.

Harriet Teare is a chemistry DPhil student at the University of Oxford

A VICIOUS CIRCLE

Dr Gerry Lawless

As an academic scientist and researcher, I am a 'producer of science', as David Perks puts it, as well as a consumer of science just like everyone else. At work, I synthesise and investigate the properties of new molecules; but at home, my family and I also have to decide on the risks of eating genetically modified foods, of our children having MMR vaccinations, or of our municipality disposing of waste by landfill or incineration.

I therefore understand keenly how the government has decided to focus on developing 'scientific literacy' rather than 'scientific training.' Indeed, I believe that a general public distrust of science in the UK is holding back scientific research that would undoubtedly benefit all of us. If science and scientists were more trusted, then more funding would be allocated by government and more science would be done.

This distrust of science is not universal. In countries where scientific endeavour has perhaps been more instrumental in improving public welfare or achieving economic power, public opinion about the role of science in society is hugely more positive. At one of our Sussex lectures, the then science minister cited an international survey that showed that fewer than 50 per cent of the British public believed that science plays a positive role in society, while the statistic in the USA was above 90 per cent.

In his comprehensive rebuttal to the government's current initiative to revamp science education at secondary school level, I would agree wholeheartedly with David Perks and much of his critique of the new GCSE curriculum for the sciences that is being launched nationwide in September 2006. It gives me pause also that this critique is being published only now, after the new curriculum has been imposed, rather than as part of a lengthy and thorough review process beforehand. I am not, however, surprised.

The new curriculum could set off a vicious circle of less thorough scientific thinking among secondary students, and therefore fewer students willing to undertake rigorous scientific research either at A-level or at degree level – and therefore fewer teachers with scientific subject degrees available to teach the next generation of students. This would derail both the government's objective of increasing general scientific literacy and its objective to encourage more economically productive scientific research. Indeed one might argue that

that circle has already begun, with the erosion in recent years of experimental skills from successive cohorts of A-level students.

Our experience at Sussex has shown that students gain an enthusiasm for science when they are allowed to get their hands dirty. When we go out to schools, we illustrate scientific principles with as many active learning techniques as we can muster. In the summer, we hold intensive week-long courses for 16-year-olds so that they can get a real taste of research in chemistry. It's like work experience for science. On our admissions days for A-level students applying to university to do chemistry, we get them into lab coats and safety glasses as quickly as possible and let them get on with experimental chemistry. They love the chance to perform in well-equipped labs, testing hypotheses about difficult problems. They appreciate the chance to be taken seriously as potential scientists.

The fact that we have had higher enrolments into our chemistry department in 2005-6 and also 2004-5 has much to do with our innovations on the typical admissions day. I have empirical evidence that enthusiasm for science comes from engaging in experiments and using the scientific method, not from simply talking about doing it. Reducing the emphasis on experimentation in the new GCSE curriculum has to be a serious flaw, and one day it could be nearly fatal for the future of Britain's historically world-class innovative science research base.

In the UK, scientific research and training is funded, primarily, at two levels. At graduate level it is funded by various panels of the Office of Science and Technology (OST), and at undergraduate level by the Higher Education Funding Council for England (HEFCE). My personal experience with government education initiatives has had more to do with the Engineering and Physical Sciences Research Council (EPSRC) and more recently with HEFCE; and in both cases, with the best will in the world, government bodies are moving in a direction that follows public opinion rather than leads it.

EPSRC funds a limited number of proposals, and prioritises them according to a perception of not only the innovation of the proposal but also the potential technological exploitation of the proposed research. Areas perceived to have fewer potential applications, and therefore less economic relevance, are less likely to be funded. The fact that many economically useful scientific advances come from research which does not target these applications specifically beforehand is an obvious truth that the funding councils do not recognise.

HEFCE's allocation of university funding is a classic example of incoherent policy. Funding is allocated, albeit with a delay, *en bloc* according to universities' perceived demand for enrolments. Thus a science student who, on average, receives circa thirty hours of tuition per week generates, for that university, 1.8 times the funding that an Arts or Humanities student secures upon receiving *circa* two hours of tuition. The increased use of market forces in the university system puts the consumer first, just as economics would prescribe. What the system does not do, however, is encourage more applicants into subjects that may be less fashionable. Eventually, a reduction in provision in these subjects becomes a *fait accompli*.

The main motivation behind the new GCSE science curriculum is to make a better informed and 'scientifically literate' population, with better problem-solving and analytical skills. On the face of it, this is not a bad objective to set. Better evaluation of scientific priorities by voters and government would be helpful for both scientists and society. However, I would have to agree strongly with David Perks' criticisms about how effective the curriculum would be in achieving this objective. Abandoning the scientific method of hypothesis, experiment, observation and conclusion for a more judgemental approach would be a great disservice to students, in my view. They would no longer have any trusted methodology for the very assessments that a judgemental, evaluative approach would ask them to make.

Is there a way to instigate instead a virtuous circle of enthused secondary students taking more science subjects at A-level and at degree level, which would flow through both to the supply of science teachers and the needs of the economy? I would suggest that the answer to the question 'What is science education for?' must undeniably be that it should educate pupils to be both intelligent consumers of science and producers of science, if that is where their intellectual interests and strengths lie. The government cannot succeed in achieving either objective if it sacrifices the training of scientists for the training of future citizens.

Dr Gerry Lawless is head of chemistry at the University of Sussex

WHAT INSPIRED ME

Craig Fairnington

When I came to make my university course choices, there was only one real option I wanted to take – physics. I am fascinated by the subject, and the decision to further my knowledge at university was the easiest I have made. According to statistics, however, this puts me in an ever-shrinking minority of school leavers; and when I look back on my science lessons at school, it is clear why many are put off.

I had a number of science teachers during my school career, and each had a different style of teaching – some manic, some painstakingly methodical – but it was always obvious, no matter how they taught, whether they were interested in the subject they were teaching. The teachers with an interest in their science made the difference between pupils grasping the concepts being taught or being baffled by streams and streams of confusing information. The teachers who knew their subject were the ones who, when asked to explain a concept again, came at it from a completely different angle, making it all so obvious.

The others, only familiar with what was laid out in the course, were more likely to carry on repeating the same old lines, verbally battering them into the pupils' minds. When it came to exams, you might remember the words taught to you, and you could mechanically apply them to a question, but it did not mean that you were able to understand what you were doing. The apathy of these teachers for the subject they were teaching passed on to pupils who had little or no real understanding of the work they were doing. When this happens, it is no surprise that these pupils do not choose to carry on studying the subject.

The best science teachers that I met while at school were the ones who knew their subject deeply, beyond the demands of coursework. They were the ones who taught in a way that made difficult concepts easier to comprehend and, more importantly, made the subject enjoyable to learn. They were able to relate the simple ideas being taught to far more impressive and complicated situations not covered by the course. It was this 'look what this leads to' attitude that made the subjects more intriguing, and encouraged myself and others to pursue science at university level.

It is clear, though, that this is not the type of teaching enjoyed by all science pupils – even through my own experience, not all teachers were like this. And when we are told that only one in five science teachers has a specialist physics qualification and only one in four chemistry teachers a specialist chemistry qualification, it is unlikely that many of these teachers have the depth of knowledge needed to engage pupils fully with science.

In a vain attempt to make science 'relevant', all that has happened is that there are now chunks of the course given over to learning that chemistry is used to help make the plastic cups you drink from, or that physics taught us how to make the light that goes on when you open the fridge. These are not exactly the best examples to give when trying to make the sciences more interesting. Far more impressive is the chemistry that creates fuels that propel the space shuttle into orbit, or the physics that allows us to see galaxies millions of light years away. While these examples are hardly relevant to school pupils' day-to-day lives, they are likely to inspire them more than plastic cups and lightbulbs do. And though these examples are more complicated, simple concepts taught in class can be related to them – especially when the teacher has the understanding needed to make the leap.

The changes made to courses to make them more relevant to pupils mean a switch to scientific examples from routine, everyday situations laid out in a mundane way, without offering any real insight or inspiration in these examples. This then confirms the ideas that many people have about science being boring and geeky, and it is difficult to overturn this mindset.

The coursework provided at our school did not leave room for many practical experiments. Whole sections of the syllabus would be worked out on the board, occasionally using a small, dreary 'safe' experiment after all this had been worked through, as if as some kind of reward. This was not just because the topic did not have any workable experiments, but was rather because of perceived safety issues. My own chemistry teacher (who had a broad background knowledge) carried out plenty of experiments not mentioned in textbooks, often with spectacular results – and this left a far greater imprint on the memory, ensuring that the concept embodied by the demonstration was remembered and understood. He struck the right balance between theory and practice, which meant that the lessons were engaging while still allowing the coursework to be learned. Other teachers simply followed the coursework, allowing the plain – often faulty – experiments to be carried out, resulting in a wasted lesson with nothing learned and nothing gained.

The reason I chose to go on and study a science at university was definitely not because of the courses I took at school. I found them largely dull and uninspiring, offering little promise of what lies ahead, and only focusing on what was needed to pass exams. My real inspiration came from teachers with a passion for science who passed that enthusiasm on, and from the popular science books that showed me the true joy of physics.

Craig Fairnington is a physics student at the University of St Andrews

NOTHING BUT FACTS?

Jonathan Kestenbaum

Innovation must flourish if the UK is to prosper in the twenty-first century. Unless, however, the number of school-leavers choosing to study the sciences at university level and beyond increases, the UK's capacity for innovation – that is both economic prosperity and the capacity to solve contemporary challenges with new solutions – will be curtailed. It is therefore imperative that the UK conducts a debate on the nature of its science education, and David Perks' essay is a challenging contribution to this process.

There is little doubt that practitioners and policy-makers across the UK now recognise that science learning must be made more engaging. This has resulted in advances in curriculum design, teacher training, professional development, and in new teaching and learning resources. NESTA has been a strong advocate of **enquiry learning** as a means of making science feel fresh and stimulating to pupils – a glorious exploration of the unknown. However, I would strongly defend these innovative forms of learning against accusations of 'dumbing down'. Indeed, many of the criticisms which surround science enquiry learning involve the creation of false dichotomies, which imply that choices have to be made between 'relevance' or scientific discipline; between the needs of the future scientist or that of the future citizen; between what pupils want to learn or what teachers and experts want them to be taught.

Enquiry learning does not necessitate these inherent distinctions, but does address the major problem currently found in science learning: that many pupils – particularly at secondary level – feel that their science education is too rushed and dominated by facts alone; that there is a lack of scope for discussion and critical debate and this can lead to indifference. At present there remains an imbalance between content and investigation, and school science tends to convey that science is about only a fixed body of known facts. As Dickens would have it in *Hard Times*:

> 'Now, what I want is, Facts. Teach these boys and girls nothing but Facts. Facts alone are wanted in life. Plant nothing else, and root out everything else. You can only form the minds of reasoning animals upon Facts: nothing else will ever be of any service to them. This is the principle on which I bring up my own children, and this is the principle on which I bring up these children. Stick to Facts, sir!'

It is, of course, absurd to suggest that such a staunchly Victorian approach is prevalent in our schools, but there does still exist an over-adherence to the importance of facts to the detriment of the skills and processes necessary to discover them – an approach which has undoubtedly contributed to increasing apathy towards the sciences in school-leavers. By giving pupils experiences that are closer to the reality of science, enquiry can encourage the capabilities and confidence to pursue further science learning, even amongst those children who are disaffected and in schools in challenging circumstances. This has strongly been the case in the educative projects invested in by NESTA over the past few years, such as *Planet Science, Digital Science and Creative Space*. The research conducted into the effectiveness of this approach has indicated that investigations and practical experiments increase motivation, develop thinking skills and support collaborative working.

Likewise, enquiry learning does not necessarily discriminate between the needs of the future scientist and those of the future citizen. At present, the lack of interest that is developing in our pupils clearly benefits neither science nor society. Enquiry learning – whereby children develop the ability to collate, synthesise and analyse empirical evidence, and to ask critical questions – provides skills and techniques which are of benefit to both. Further, boosting scientific literacy in the general public – which will increasingly become as important as literacy and numeracy in an ever more technically advanced society – will be achieved through investigation, experimentation or the testing of hypotheses. A strengthening of the understanding of these processes, even at a basic level, and including the uncertainties of these processes, might help to support a more informed and critical engagement with potentially contentious areas of research. Indeed, it could be argued that they are fundamental to active citizenship in a highly technological society.

Yet in putting the case for increased science enquiry learning, it must be made clear that this is not something to be imposed upon an unwilling teaching profession. Both teachers and pupils want science education to involve high-quality content delivered in an engaging and stimulating manner. Last year a NESTA-commissioned poll of 500 secondary school teachers from across the UK found that the 84 per cent considered science enquiry learning to be very important – with 87 per cent agreeing that it can have a significant impact on pupils' performance. Significantly, however, 64 per cent stated that they found themselves curtailed by a lack of time and resources, and 87 per cent also said that they had at least once prevented their students from undertaking practical work because they believed current health and safety regulations prohibit them from doing so.

There is a sufficient degree of flexibility within the current National Curriculum for more innovative learning schemes to be developed, and central government must offer greater encouragement to schools and teachers to facilitate the prevalence of such methods of teaching. Across educational establishments, knowledge-sharing networks to spread particular models of learning which have delivered successful outcomes – after proper evaluation of their impact and outcomes – must be developed in order to share good practice. This could involve the introduction of dedicated project managers into schools, making links to topics beyond the traditional science curriculum and securing the commitment of senior management within schools.

The debate around science education and how best to equip the UK for the challenges ahead will continue to rage. However, I am convinced that the innovative, practical methods of learning found within science enquiry offer the greatest opportunity to both arrest the present fall in student numbers and, importantly, maintain pupils' knowledge and understanding of core scientific principles and standards.

Jonathan Kestenbaum is chief executive of NESTA, the National Endowment for Science, Technology and the Arts

AN ELITIST POSITION

Ian Mellor

David Perks' essay on the new science curriculum, its origins and its effects, rings bells across the whole panorama of education.

It is not physics alone that is short of serious high-calibre students: that is true of almost all the traditional 'hard' subjects that once constituted the diet of the nation's brightest children. Maths has been complaining of declining numbers for years. Modern languages have tried to counter the trend by easing the intellectual content of their A-levels considerably, and will be hit further once the drop in GCSE candidates (that became apparent in 2006) move on to A-levels in 2008.

But even when the factual and intellectual content of chemistry has been constrained, it still does not offset students' awareness that subjects like chemistry are harder than many other subjects; while what has to matter for students at ages 16 and 18, for most practical purposes, is a fistful of top grades, regardless of the subjects in which they are achieved and the manner in which those subjects award the grades.

The fact that virtually worthless courses in scientific literacy should burgeon in this climate is not surprising: indeed, it is a logical stage in the development of education in its present form. There is nothing ultra-new about the lack of 'hard subject' graduates – ask any headteacher who has been trying to recruit teachers, and especially young ones, for these subjects and you will be told that a) recruitment is extremely difficult; and b) those who present themselves bring a far more limited subject knowledge to the classroom than do teachers brought up twenty years ago on more traditional syllabuses.

Indeed, it is already highly probable that a child in a state school is being taught science by non-specialists. It is not even guaranteed that an examination marker in physics is a specialist: in 2005 my own school's GCSE candidates were disturbed to discover, as revealed by the examiner's comments on their coursework, that the examiner knew less physics than they did. This is nothing less than scandalous. It is bad enough not to be able to recruit knowledgeable people to teach; it is even worse to have examination judgements made by such people. An entitlement to separate sciences, even for a so-called 'elite' section of the pupil body, would create in many schools an insoluble problem.

It is certainly not right to allow the preferences and opinions of the pupils to dictate the curriculum. Most do not have the maturity to see where their rejection of hard subjects and especially of meaningful science will lead them as individuals, or the nation as a whole. Were we to take that process to its logical conclusion, we might easily sit all day in a sandpit or in front of computer games. Only from the elite group of academic pupils might one glean useful feedback for curricular consideration – but the bulk of the nation might be surprised by their demand for a broader and less anglicised history course, for greater learning through practical work and experiments, and also for the general re-introduction of Latin.

It must be admitted that teachers have remained relatively silent throughout the dumbing down processes of the past fifteen years or so, maintaining a stoic front but sadly keeping quiet in the face of the nonsensical innovations of AS and A2. Those of us who recall that AS was originally a device for rendering meaningful the year of post-GCSE study (which a proportion of students undertook before abandoning their education) understand why AS/A2 was constructed as it was, and why the syllabuses – sorry, specifications – and the testing were shaped as they were.

Over and above the direct interventions of universities, schools, teachers, parents and pupils lies the hand of government, of whatever hue. The present one trumpeted the cause of education and, laudably, set out to improve levels of literacy and numeracy. But in the world of politics it is not what is actually achieved but the sourcing of statistics to present the effects of your interventions in the best possible light that really matters.

League tables, whether the lists of detailed percentages offered by the government or the arrantly foolish quasi-sporting leagues developed by the media, have come to dictate all manner of educational practice. Their value to the pupils is undeniable: top grades have become demonstrably far easier to get by a variety of means, ranging from watered-down syllabuses through facile testing methods to straightforward lowering (even the abandonment) of traditional standards. Government decrees have exacerbated the problem, driven once more by the need to prove that its interventions have worked: nothing shows this more clearly than the ludicrous tables of GCSE equivalences, according to which various culinary or musical grades are worth anything from two to four GCSE passes in physics, chemistry, Latin, German and other such 'hard' subjects. The intention was originally a laudable one: to provide, where it was needed, a credible value for vocational courses as against academic ones. But the net result has been a fall in English and maths grades, set against a rise in overall passes generated by the likes of cake-decoration.

What is more – and this is crucial to the debate about the new scientific literacy syllabus – even those students emerging with high GCSE grades in the separate sciences, languages, and history, to name but a few, are by no means guaranteed success if they continue to A-level. Transition from O-level to A-level, then to S-level and on to university, used not to be a major issue. Now it is. If only I had a pound for every disappointed parent to whom I have explained that an A* in any given subject at GCSE is no guarantee of a top grade at A-level! Similarly, universities are highly conscious these days of having to teach large chunks of knowledge and skills which at one time could be taken for granted in an 18-year-old with AAB or better.

With nothing beyond scientific literacy – and that at A* – pupils are going to have no basis at all for an A-level and/or university education in science to anything approaching a useful standard. The reasons are the need to perpetuate a self-justifying set of statistics, the form of examinations, especially those based on modules, and the lowering of standards so as to accommodate a decent proportion of the weakest candidates in a range twice as great as it once was.

If I condemn the notion of this scientific literacy adventure, I do so based on naked elitism. A large proportion of any nation's population will never be nuclear scientists – though, as an aside, it is astonishing how many Hong Kong pupils are stretched to become very capable junior scientists and mathematicians merely as a result of high expectations. But a nation needs to educate to a high standard those who are inherently capable of reaching that standard: without high achievers there will be no option but to import scientists of quality, and that into a society increasingly conditioned to distrust anyone of significant intellectual capacity.

'Elitism' is a word much bandied in this context, and it is always used pejoratively. I hardly need to ask what a Britain without elite minds will be like; and it will be futile to blame 'elite' schools for breeding social distinctions – the job will have been done by scientific literacy and other such misguided forms of education.

Ian Mellor is former head of Stockport Grammar School

WORK WITH THE INDEPENDENT SECTOR

Steve Hearn

I left the state education system in 1985 to teach physics in an independent school. I just wanted to teach physics. For the past twenty years I have tried to teach the subject in an exciting and engaging way. Examples of 'how science works' are always included in my teaching plans. I use practical investigations for education, to give insight into the scientific method, and at the same time to encourage the development of communication skills. I make visits with pupils to universities and industry and invite scientists into the classroom to talk to my students.

Curriculum fashions have come and gone. I have seen many, and ignored most of them. Assessment and terminal examinations have not profoundly influenced the education process in my classroom. Many will dismiss my comments above with the comment that an independent school is an ivory tower, where you do not have to work hard. So be it.

The facts recently reported by Alan Smithers and Pamela Robinson, in their report *Physics in schools and universities 2: Patterns and Policies* are deeply disturbing. They noted that students in independent and grammar schools 'are more likely to take A-level physics' than those in the state sector, and that since 1990, 'entries for A-level physics have fallen by 35 per cent'[1]. Many have commented on the implications of this report. Analysis of the statistics shows that the decline in uptake of physics at A-level is linked to a lack of specialist physics teachers working in the state system.

In May 2002 prime minister Tony Blair, speaking to the Royal Society, stated: 'We also need to deepen school specialisation in science, in particular by seeking new forms of collaboration involving colleges and higher education institutions.'[2] Tony Blair has probably made more statements about the importance of science and scientists to the future economic security of our country than any other prime minister. I think that he is correct in this belief. I suspect also that the concept of collaboration between maintained schools and other institutions is an important one.

I am convinced that the new curriculum will have a positive effect. Twenty First Century Science is an impressive piece of work, and learning about how science works will for the majority of pupils be an exciting and welcome change. There are plenty of good science

1   *Physics in schools and universities 2: Patterns and Policies*, Alan Smithers and Pamela Robinson, Centre for Education and Employment, University of Buckingham, August 2006

2   Tony Blair, Speech to the Royal Society, 23 May 2002

teachers in post who can deliver the new curriculum. And with the support of the Science Learning Centres network and the availability of high quality continuing professional development (CPD) for the first time in our profession, I do not fear for the majority of pupils studying science. Most pupils will benefit from its approach and content.

What about that minority of potential serious scientists? Those who might want to study physics at university, for example? I want to focus now on what I shall call the 'physics problem': that we have too few physics graduates in post in state schools.

As a result of the Department for Education and Skills (DfES) scheme to encourage state independent partnerships, and because of my work as an Institute of Physics teacher network co-ordinator, I have built up a considerable knowledge and experience of physics education at GCSE and A-level in maintained schools and teacher training institutions. The problem concerning the lack of young graduate physics teachers in post was clear to me before the publication of the Smithers and Robinson report. A physics specialist is needed to encourage and nurture the development of the future physicist, and such a person is in short supply in the maintained sector.

Over the next few years, while government deals with the ramifications of the Smithers and Robinson report, what will happen to the significant number of potential physicists in maintained schools? I am not suggesting that all state schools are struggling to find physics graduate teachers – but a significant fraction of maintained schools are. I am not suggesting physics teaching is poor in state schools: I know in general it is not. But there is something missing in physics lessons in many schools.

Unless some intervention strategy is developed right now, the 'physics problem' will undoubtedly worsen. We will produce an even smaller number of physics graduates, fewer physicists for industry, and maybe none at all for teaching. Physics at GCSE and A-level may disappear from state schools. This would be an educational catastrophe of monumental proportions.

As an independent school teacher, every year I have a large number of A-level physics candidates – some of whom, by the way, have come to A-level via dual award science and not separate subject GCSEs. Every year a few study physics, three or four out of 50 or 60.

One pupil in 20 years has gone on to teach physics. Early on I thought, 'what is this "physics problem" they are talking about?' Then it became clear as I, too, found it hard to find physics graduates to teach in my department.

What I would like to see created, supported and actively resourced by the government as soon as possible is a more extensive state/independent partnership scheme. If an independent physics department, comparatively rich in material and manpower resources, committed two hours to help with the education of local maintained pupils who think they might want to go on to study physics in more depth, it could have a tremendous impact on the lives of those pupils.

It is easy to view such a proposal cynically. I don't see it as a patronising exercise where the independent sector is creaming off the best pupils, the brightest and easiest to teach. I don't see this as a scheme where the state school teacher is being rescued by the independent sector 'expert'. The focus of the partnership scheme would be on helping to develop the minority of state pupils who might want to be serious physics students. In schools where physics expertise is needed, I am proposing a scheme to meet the demand, at least partially.

We, as a country, need to do whatever it takes to achieve this goal. A real partnership approach would see non-physicist state teachers working with the independent specialists. Partnerships are hard to develop and maintain, but there are many benefits for schools that are prepared to work together. In many cases the state teacher could lead the lesson, drawing upon the independent teacher as a consultant. Maintained sector pupils would gain access to support and resources that they might not have had access to under the present system. Some might even end up studying physics at university.

How to teach and what to teach are, in my view, easy problems to solve. There are plenty of organisations and support networks out there to help with these tasks. The curriculum is really not the issue. But the 'physics problem' looks more difficult. While governments toil earnestly to solve this problem, a significant number of state school pupils will miss out on the opportunity to study physics at university. A-level physics education may become the exclusive responsibility of independent schools. Surely this is an unacceptable state of affairs, in a country with our scientific heritage and pedigree?

Steve Hearn is former head of science and physics at Charterhouse School

WHAT A RESEARCH INSTITUTE CAN CONTRIBUTE

Dr Michael Sargent

At a time when scientific progress is seen as an important motor of the economy, the scientific community has an important stake in science teaching in schools. The purpose of this article is to reflect upon how this community can contribute to the advancement of science in schools, and specifically to reflect upon our experiences at the National Institute for Medical Research (NIMR) over more than a decade.

A key lesson has been that contacts with schools can be fragile and elusive because of the very high turnover of staff and the frenetic atmosphere inspired by educational reforms. While our events are always oversubscribed, this peculiar problem is a warning for anyone developing enrichment activities. Our principle activities include 'Schools Days', a Summer School for Research, an essay competition and a commitment to help our young scientists contribute to teaching in schools through the Ambassadors for Science scheme.

Not everyone agrees that our Annual Schools Days are useful. A teacher from a prominent girls' grammar school describes our activities as 'a complete waste of time', because we 'do not follow the syllabus'. Notwithstanding this contra-indication we find our programmes – talks, demonstrations, a quiz and discussion about science, careers or ethical issues – are valued by students and teachers. We have learnt that for the event to be interesting and memorable, the audience must be led into unfamiliar territory carefully and without lab jargon. Our younger staff seem to manage this instinctively and more effectively than silver-tongued stars of the professional firmament.

Teachers generally appreciate accessible talks about unfamiliar topics (such as new developments in stem cell research, immunology or developmental biology) and like to hear a synoptic overview of important subjects. In a small way this corresponds to the 'professional development' advocated by the Wellcome Trust. In the Wellcome Trust's view, interest in science as a university subject or career is significantly enhanced by the ability of teachers to project the essential interest and importance of science. The Trust has established that 73 per cent of science teachers believe they need additional subject-specific training. [1] To facilitate this Wellcome, in collaboration with the Department for Education and Skills (DfES), has provided a £51 million investment in a network of centres capable of delivering 9000 training days a year. [2] This is unlikely to become routine

1 'Believers, Seekers and Sceptics: What teachers think about continuing professional development', Wellcome Trust, 2005

2 Evidence to the House of Lords Enquiry into School Science, Wellcome Trust, 2006

for some years, as teachers are unlikely to be free to attend courses unless an external source pays for supply cover, and so on. In the meanwhile academia has a useful role.

NIMR's Summer School, underwritten by the Nuffield Foundation, is an intense experience of research for an elite group of students drawn from as many local schools as possible. Academics without experience of the scheme, and school teachers too, may wonder what a 17-year-old with no relevant knowledge can do in four weeks. When so much is required of supervisors it is pleasing that they find the effort worthwhile. We find that after four weeks these highly motivated students have a fine report and an attractive poster to show at school and other events. Back at school the impact is significant. Posters are usually displayed prominently; the students make a presentation to their class-mates; another year group becomes interested or even inspired, and the curiosity of teachers is aroused by their efforts.

Most public discussion of 'enrichment activities' is about what 'we' can do for students, but a neglected topic is what students can do to help themselves. Participation in the Nuffield Bursary scheme reveals one kind of determination, but through our Human Biology Essay Competition we are successfully involving more students in 'scholarship'. The idea that a 16-17 year old will enter an essay competition voluntarily may seem unlikely, but in the third and fourth year of the competition we had a total of more than 200 entries, originating from across the entire educational spectrum. With intriguing essay titles we hope to start a life-long enthusiasm for science and the written word at a time when science students rarely write an extended essay before they go to university. We are really challenging schools to be more ambitious for their brightest students, and we do get a significant amount of help from some teachers who encourage their students to enter. The bait is a financial prize and a day spent at NIMR for the best three; and for everyone who participates there is the current volume of Mill Hill Essays with a certificate demonstrating their participation in the competition.

Enterprising schemes for encouraging young scientists to participate in teaching their subject in schools are now in operation. Many schools remain unaware of the merits of the 'Ambassadors for Science' or 'Researchers in Residence', who might give one afternoon a week over one term to a school. Quite a number of young NIMR staff have been welcomed by schools and given the opportunity to make sparky contributions, engaging in activities that range from 'revision lessons' for examination classes to incisive presentations based on their expertise at all levels.

The above examples show how a smallish organisation can provide scientific enrichment activities for schools. We have little feel for the global issues, but we can identify a few problems based on our rather subjective experiences, in addition to the difficulty of maintaining open communications with schools. Most obvious is the ignorance that prevails about potential careers in science and the value of a science education to society. It is extremely difficult to convey to 16-year-olds the texture of many careers. Medicine and law require relatively little imagination, especially if a school makes them seem a feasible ambition, together with the knowledge that a highly developed training scheme will fill in the gaps. This makes an established profession seem a safe and sensible choice, even without considering the adequacy of remuneration; it takes a lot more imagination to visualise the life of a scientist.

When science students arrive at university they probably rarely reflect on the fate of their peer group, which will, in thirty years' time, become a remarkably diverse group. Collectively it will include professors, research directors, business people, patent inspectors, freelance inventors, important public servants, industrial managers, experts on thousands of issues great and small, science writers, teachers and technicians; all grounded in the scientific method. Some of them will make revolutionary contributions that change the face of science and society, while others will make pots of money from astute use of the possibilities of science. A large and important group will develop special interests in a scientific subject that will make them valued employees in a variety of organisations. None of these futures is in any way pre-ordained; science changes so fast that almost nobody can predict what will happen ten years from now.

The progress of science internationally is assured. But in Britain there is an anxiety that our efforts will be eclipsed by other nations – perhaps precipitated, some say, by the declining quality of our graduates. To blame this on schools seems a little unfair, when failures at university level or in the proper ambition of venture capitalists are just as plausible a cause. It is worth remembering that in the early days of the biotechnology revolution, important British contributions and capacities were not exploited through lack of imagination by venture capitalists and others.

A comment by the Confederation of British Industry (CBI) encapsulates another problem: 'it makes economic sense to source science graduates ... from China and India' [3]. The language is evocative of a project manager looking for bags of cement rather than for highly trained, creative individuals. What are employers doing to make science seem less bland and unappealing? The decline in numbers of children doing sciences at A-level is in part fuelled by the availability of softer subjects in which they can score high grades easily. Possibly the goal posts should be moved to put all subjects on an equal footing. The Bioscience Federation warns that the pool of mainstream biologists qualified to teach A-level biology to a high standard is falling steadily. [4] Apparently, biology students are being diverted into specialised areas such as sports science, psychology and forensic science.

The Wellcome Trust and other organisations are very active in supporting and encouraging teachers to do the best for their students. The place of a relatively powerless organisation, such as NIMR, is to provide the best enrichment activities we can. Over the entire country there is a need for much more, and it behoves scientists everywhere to pull their weight; it is no use whingeing about the quality of students if scientists do nothing to help.

Dr Michael Sargent, National Institute for Medical Research

3 'UK looking overseas for science graduates', *Guardian*, March 16th 2006

4 Evidence to the House of Lords Enquiry into School Science, Bioscience Federation, 2006

WAIT FOR THE EVIDENCE

Helen O'Brien

The introduction of the new science GCSEs in autumn 2006 has been described as the biggest change to school science since the introduction of the national curriculum in 1988. It is going to affect all 14-year-olds in the country – from this September, they have no option but to follow a scientific literacy-based curriculum through to GCSE level.

'The aim is to maintain and increase interest in science as a subject', according to the Qualifications and Curriculum Authority (QCA). But is giving science a context and methodology the best use of the available teaching time? And is it right to implement a complete change of direction for science teaching before the independent evaluations of trials have been completed?

A SCIENTIFICALLY LITERATE POPULATION

This country needs scientifically literate citizens. Even if some are quite happy to go through life not wanting to question the origins of the universe, or investigate how a telephone works, they cannot escape the impact that science and technology have on everyday life. From the application of new medical techniques to the problems of climate change, advances in science and technology affect almost everything we do.

A good grasp of scientific principles is essential to navigate effectively through life. So the question then becomes, how do you give kids a grasp of scientific principles? Through studying the basics of science, discussing contemporary issues in a science context, or looking at how science works?

How do you go about answering the question 'Would you give your child the MMR vaccine?' Pupils today have unimaginable resources in the form of the internet. They can find out what sparked the story, how the media reported it, and what Andrew Wakefield wrote in his article for the Lancet. They can find out what type of research led Dr Wakefield to his conclusions – that it was a preliminary study that had not been peer reviewed, and that it involved 12 children. Does the circumstantial evidence of parents noticing a change in the behaviour in 8 of the children at the time when they had the MMR vaccine suggest a causal link with the vaccine itself?

But studying science should not just be another branch of media studies. To get to the informed answer, students need the background in science – how a vaccine works, how diseases are passed on. They also need some appreciation of the complex terminology used by scientists, and the methodology of science: for example, how do you conduct a clinical trial and how large should the sample size be?

SCIENCE FOR SCIENTISTS

In addition to a scientifically literate population, we also need to train future scientists. Science has so much going for it – the chance to find cures for cancer, design safer, faster trains, or find the solutions to the looming energy crisis. So why is there a decline in the numbers of science and technology graduates?

The good news is that science is now compulsory for all 14-16 year olds. There is no longer an option to 'disapply' or opt out of science. Science teachers have a captive audience. But the bad news is that most of that captive audience disappears when given the chance, at age 16.

WHERE ARE THE PHYSICISTS?

Does science have an image problem? It seems the problem is not with science but with physics. Biology is booming – it was the fourth most popular A-level subject in summer 2006 (behind English, general studies and maths), and psychology was challenging history for fifth place. Chemistry is waning but still attracted over 40,000 A-level applicants. It is physics that is in decline, with only half as many budding physicists as potential biologists.

Perhaps using current affairs to trigger debates about science in the classroom can play a valuable role in helping children visualise themselves as future scientists. But the majority of science media stories concern health issues. Space missions do get the occasional mention, but engineering rarely gets a look in. Perhaps discussing the MMR vaccine and bird flu can help kids see themselves as doctors or medical researchers, but biology is already a popular subject. There are not too many media stories concerning magnetic fields, or mechanics or radiation (except in a medical context). If we are not careful, in the interests of making science relevant we could end up making physics seem even less so.

What if teenagers are not studying A-level physics because they just can't see themselves as future physicists? Not because it is too hard, or too boring, but because it has ceased to seem relevant to students who want to further social justice by becoming lawyers, for example?

The fact that A-level physics, requiring high levels of abstract and analytical thought, is one of the most rigorous and profound of all the subjects is not what we have trained our teenagers to see. Physics is not just about aspiring to become the next Albert Einstein or Stephen Hawking and grapple with the big questions of the origins of the universe. Physicists and engineers can also have an impact on social justice through providing cheap and efficient energy supplies to Africa; they can change the world by figuring out just how climate change is going to affect the weather systems of the globe. There are still 50,000 students taking maths A-level, so they are clearly not scared off by abstract concepts and equations *per se*.

Isambard Kingdom Brunel made it to second place in the BBC's recent Great Britons competition. Engineering can be perceived as great (although this probably had a lot to do with the passionate arguments put forward by Jeremy Clarkson).

I think we do all three science subjects a disservice by merging them into a single or dual award. How about treating physics seriously and promoting it back to its proper place as a subject in its own right? And making sure we find some more teachers to do a Jeremy Clarkson – teachers who were inspired enough to study physics to A-level and degree level themselves?

WHY THE HURRY?

Perhaps the most worrying part of the introduction of the new GCSE is not that experts in science education want to try something new: one size rarely fits all in education, and most people welcome different approaches to suit different teaching styles and schools. A bigger concern is that the decision has been taken to implement the new curriculum across the board before the results of the school trial have been fully evaluated. Two independent reports into the implementation of the new curriculum and the response to it by teachers and children are due to be published by the end of 2006.

Here is a possible question for the new GCSE science: A pilot study for the new Twenty First Century Science GCSEs has been running in 75 schools for the past three years. A report compiled at the end of the first year of the trial, based on visits to 7 of the schools and questionnaires returned from 40 schools, concludes that the new GCSEs were broadly welcomed by teachers and students. Is this sufficient evidence to roll out the curriculum across the country?

This is a nervous time for science. Whether the gamble to change the approach to teaching science will pay off and provide scientifically literate citizens and future Nobel laureates remains to be seen.

Helen O'Brien is an instrumentation engineer at the Space Magnetometer Laboratory at Imperial College London

A LACK OF SELF-BELIEF

Dr Peter Martin

David Perks is right to argue that the reform of GCSE science to promote 'scientific literacy' is detrimental to the dual challenge of educating new generations of inspired scientists and improving science education across the whole population. When I took my first academic post, after nine years of post-compulsory education and a further three years of post-doctoral research, I felt that I had finally become fluent enough in science to craft and manage my own research projects. Scientific literacy is not something which came easily to me.

As a university lecturer, I devote much of my time to helping undergraduate engineering science students achieve an understanding of the past 20-odd centuries of science and its application. By the end of their four years of study, and in particular after they have conducted a year-long independent research project, most of our students have begun to appreciate some of the uncertainties and contradictions which exist in specific areas of scientific knowledge. For the more able students, the regime of post-graduate study is then open for them to explore, understand and work on resolving some of these. These are the labours which enable people to achieve genuine scientific literacy, or, in other words, to become scientists.

As Perks discusses, a central assumption of the scientific literacy reform is that only a minority of pupils are likely to want to go on to study science seriously and possibly become scientists. Proponents of reform see traditional science education as being aimed at just this minority. It may have been successful for a few, but, they argue, it has left the majority disenfranchised, bored and labelled as failures. The teaching of scientific literacy is something which they think all pupils may achieve success in, whilst safeguarding the separate sciences for the minority whom they think want to study science. Perks does a good job of challenging the 'relevance' agenda and of making the case for scientific content to be put into the heart of GCSE sciences for all. One feature which I think bears further scrutiny is the assurance that this reform does not represent a threat to the teaching of separate science GCSEs, or for those who want to go on to be scientists.

Reformers propose that pupils who are likely to become the next generation of scientists may still study separate sciences, in addition to scientific literacy. Furthermore, they argue that the increase in pupil engagement through their courses will lead to more students wanting to study sciences at a higher level. However, in my experience, the trends that Perks argues have been detrimental to GCSE science are all-pervasive, even at the highest levels of education. All science education is affected, whether it is taught to an elite and or the majority.

As well as being the oldest English-speaking university in the world, Oxford University also has possibly the most intensive undergraduate tutoring in the world. Typically, students will have two hours of tutoring each week in small groups of one or two students. These are undertaken by college tutors, who double as lecturers in the university departments. These tutorials are in addition to the lecturing, laboratories and classes held in the department. This gives an unparalleled opportunity for academics to engage with their students on the higher conceptual problems of their subject. With academics often tutoring a broad range of subjects, rather than just their specialist areas, it also lends the university a truly scholarly atmosphere.

At first we are faced with practical obstacles to making the most of this special opportunity. For example, pressure from sources such as the Quality Assurance Agency (QAA) has instigated a series of bureaucratic measures. Examples include the promotion of course syllabuses and lecture notes to follow the syllabus. Whilst these may improve the measurable service provision of the university, they serve to impair scientific learning. The vast body of scientific knowledge, and the skill of how to use it, is divided up into prescribed chunks with no encouragement for students to stray outside their bounds. The production of immaculate lecture notes leaves students with little encouragement to read textbooks and stretch their understanding. Hungry to maximise degree performance, students are provoked to ask: 'Do we have to know this?'

Further problems come with the gulf between students' school experiences and our expectations of them at university. The expectation of mastering a whole subject in one go has been stripped from science A-levels. The ability of the new intake to think conceptually about a problem, rather than just try to find the answer, can seem alien to them. Our tutorials have long been based on question sheets, designed to guide and test students' thought. However, rather than being an aid to reach higher understanding, I admit that the set questions can become a focus of my tutorials, with students pressing for textbook answers to be delivered on the whiteboard.

It is a challenge for tutors to combat these trends, to shape our students into the best thinkers that they can be and get them to master their discipline. We work through our everyday tutoring and lecturing to tackle these practical problems. Over the years of study, this builds up to the final point where the student can prove his or her mastery through university examination. Hence, the name 'Finals' is given to our university exams, which provide a demanding and definitive summative assessment of a student and his or her authority in a discipline. However, whilst we make all this effort we find that the carpet is being pulled from beneath our feet.

The fundamental concept of assessing a student based on his or her final understanding of a discipline is under threat. For example, in the 2004 QAA audit of Oxford University, the Department of Physics is 'encouraged' to 'give further consideration to widening its methods of assessment so as to incorporate student achievement in practical work and coursework into the overall degree classification'. The Department of Engineering Science is pressed to 'consider how its strategy for summative assessment might better recognise the full range of student achievement and skills'. Such pressure has resulted in the Departments of Chemistry and Physics dropping Finals to introduce second-year university examinations in addition to those at the end of the final year.

The basic conception of the academic scientist is based on the combined notions that disciplining nature yields knowledge, and that disciplined study masters knowledge. The fragmentation of scientific disciplines in university courses damages their integrity. This is symptomatic of a wider questioning of the validity of having scientific disciplines. For example in 2005, Sir Howard Newby, former chief executive of the Higher Education Funding Council for England, hit the headlines by saying that it was both inevitable and desirable that what he called 'nineteenth-century' subjects – the sciences such as maths, chemistry, physics, engineering and biology – should face closures as the demand for new hybrid subjects grows.

This is unfortunate because undermining subject disciplines has the effect of undermining scientific authority – it takes away what makes scientists special. A lack of self-belief in what we understand disables us from demanding that students prove themselves to us. We merely become service providers in the education industry.

This trend is expressed through the uptake of Problem Based Learning (PBL) in many universities, especially in the sciences. PBL elevates the process of learning over content. Academic scholars are relegated to facilitators, as Perks similarly described with teachers. I'm all in favour of encouraging students to study inventively off their own back and to learn from their peers, but PBL removes the prize of this study – the conquest of an academic discipline.

There is no one who clearly stands to gain from this process. As Perks argues, this trend is representative of a society which has become ambivalent towards the authority of science and knowledge. This will increasingly pose problems, and has had serious consequences already. For example, David Ball, professor of risk management at Middlesex University, in 2005 felt compelled to resign from the government's Committee on Radioactive Waste Management, stating that it had become obsessed with public consultation at the expense of expert scientific advice.

Perks quotes *Beyond 2000*'s innocuous-sounding statement that 'the ever-growing importance of scientific issues in our daily lives demands a populace who have sufficient knowledge and understanding to follow science and scientific debates'. In today's climate, it is not the growing importance of science in our lives which precipitates these debates. Rather, it is the degradation of scientific authority which precipitates them and allows them to rumble on. I agree with Perks' thesis; to promote genuine scientific literacy we must uphold the status of the academic disciplines and get pupils to study them.

Dr Peter Martin is a lecturer in the department of engineering at the University of Oxford

The initial impetus for this project was to take a critical look at science education in general. However, the government's reform of the 14-16 science curriculum made focusing on the new GCSE curriculum the perfect exemplar of broader trends in science education. As I write, the Qualifications and Curriculum Authority (QCA) has just published its revised criteria for A-level science subjects. Scientific literacy has found itself embedded into A-level science subjects, with the mandatory inclusion of 'How science works' within each of the new science specifications. Marianne Cutler, executive director of professional and curriculum innovation at the Association for Science Education (ASE), said that she expects that science teachers would also applaud the requirement that pupils must be taught to 'appreciate the ways in which society uses science to inform decision-making'.

Some of us beg to differ. The fact that this publication has attracted comments from such a wide range of contributors is testament to the unease about the direction in which science education is going, and gives the lie to the idea that there is a universal consensus over the current reforms. I hope that the debate within these pages will at the very least give us the opportunity to air our concerns before the position becomes irrevocable, and I am very grateful to everyone who has taken the time to contribute.

One theme that has emerged, both in the contributions to this publication and in the discussions leading up to it, is a certain loss of faith in what we can achieve with science education. Some assume a bipolar approach to the purpose of science education, where the aim of education is either to empower tomorrow's citizens or to nurture future scientists. For example, Simon Singh clearly prioritises the future scientist, whilst Michael Reiss makes a substantive case for the citizen being the major focus of science education. Both approaches fall short of answering the question 'What is science education for?'

I have argued that science education should aim to give all young people an appreciation of what we know about the natural world. It should be an education in science and nothing else.

Despite Simon Singh's obvious passion for physics, I cannot help feeling that his argument that we should focus our efforts on students with a 'strong aptitude for science' reflects a loss of faith in our ability to engage increasing numbers of young people in a subject he finds both fascinating and immensely important to the modern world. To retreat into a position where only a small minority of pupils receive an academic science education is an admission of defeat.

However, several contributors adopt a similar perspective, in expressing a willingness to accept a focus on scientific literacy for the majority if it means the minority of potential future scientists can be guaranteed a sound academic education. Have we really gone so far as to give up any hope of communicating science to increasing numbers of 14-16 years olds? How will we determine who belongs in the future scientific elite?

Other contributors, such as Andrew Hunt and Michael Reiss, seem intent on pursuing science education through a focus on the citizen. But their view of the citizen falls somewhat short of my own. In their view, the citizen is in need of education about the pros and cons of using science to solve the technological problems we face in society. Hunt is an advocate of science, but he does not seem to think it important for all young people to study science. In the compulsory core component of the Twenty First Century Science GCSE course, the emphasis is placed on studying the impact of science on our lives rather than on science as an academic discipline. Reiss is keen to educate the citizen in 'criticality' by, for instance, debating the pros and cons of nuclear power. But as Mary Warnock points out, this kind of approach is 'less science than morals and politics'.

For all Hunt's protestations that traditional science teaching is boring, I fail to see how pandering in the classroom to existing prejudices about the dangers of science and technology is going to give science a bigger hold on young people's imagination. A diet of topical issues, from obesity to mobile phones, is neither new to schools nor engaging for young people. Like the trite storylines in EastEnders that push the latest message about parenting or drugs, science lessons will become repetitive and dull. Could there be anything more likely to turn young people off science? Surely, if we believe science is important enough, we should be able to get the idea across without dressing it up like a second-rate soap opera or TV chat show?

If we believe it is important that young people appreciate science, then we should believe young people are capable of learning what we choose to tell them about the natural world.

As Craig Fairnington, an 18-year-old student about to start a physics degree at St Andrews University, put it: 'The best science teachers that I met while at school were the ones who knew their subject deeply.' Like Fairnington, I believe the best way to get science across to young people is to leave it to teachers with a passion for their subject. If allowed to develop their craft, good teachers can find a way of communicating even complicated scientific concepts to young minds. It may not always work, but surely it is better to try than to give up before we have even started?

BIOGRAPHIES

Craig Fairnington

Craig Fairnington has recently completed his studies at Harris Academy, Dundee, where he studied maths, physics, chemistry and computing in his sixth year. He has just begun his undergraduate studies in physics at the University of St Andrews. Fairnington was the winner of the best individual award in the Institute of Ideas' Debating Matters competition 2006. His inspiration for studying physics was reading John Gribbin's *In Search of Schrödinger's Cat* at age 15.

Dr Eliot Forster

Eliot Forster is a graduate of the University of Liverpool, where he gained a BSc and PhD in neurophysiology; he also has an MBA from Henley Management College. He has lived and worked in Liverpool, London, Groton (Connecticut) and Sandwich, Kent. He is now VP of Pfizer Global Research & Development (PGRD), Site Head of Development at its Sandwich Laboratories and Head of Development Operations in Europe and Asia. Forster is a board director of a health consortium assembled by the South East England Development Agency (SEEDA) to help promote and expand life sciences in the region. He also works with several universities to support their enterprise activities. Forster has three children and, outside of work, has an active interest in politics, running, food and wine.

Tony Gilland

Tony Gilland is science and society director at the Institute of Ideas in London. He has programmed a number of events on scientific and medical controversies. Gilland has written widely on the problem of risk aversion and defensiveness about scientific experimentation, and is a frequent guest on radio and television programmes in the UK. He is currently the national coordinator of the Institute's acclaimed Debating Matters competition for sixth form students: www.debatingmatters.com. He holds a degree in Philosophy, Politics and Economics from the University of Oxford.

Steve Hearn

Steve Hearn is an Institute of Physics network co-ordinator for Surrey, and a teacher fellow of the Science Enhancement Project. He is former head of science and physics at Charterhouse School.

Andrew Hunt

Andrew Hunt is director of the Nuffield Curriculum Centre and co-director of the Twenty First Century Science project. Hunt taught science for 20 years in secondary modern, comprehensive and grammar schools. He is an experienced textbook author and curriculum developer, and has a particular interest in courses to develop scientific literacy and in chemistry education. Hunt is president of the London region of the Association for Science Education and active in the ASE's 'Science across the World' project. For further information see: www.nuffieldcurriculumcentre.org.

Dr Brian Iddon MP

Dr Brian Iddon MP, BSc, PhD, DSc, FRSC, CChem, graduated at Hull University and has taught chemistry at Durham and Salford Universities. He is a visiting professor in the department of chemistry at Liverpool University, an adviser to the school of chemistry at Manchester University, and Chairman of the Board of Bolton Technical Innovation Centre Ltd. Iddon received honorary membership of the Society of Chemical Industry in 2003, an honorary fellowship of the University of Bolton in 2005, and the President's Award from the Royal Society of Chemistry in 2006. Brian Iddon was elected as a Member of Parliament for Bolton South East in 1997, and was re-elected in 2001 and 2005.

Jonathan Kestenbaum

Jonathan Kestenbaum is chief executive of NESTA, the National Endowment for Science, Technology and the Arts. Previously he was Chief of Staff to Sir Ronald Cohen, the Chairman of Apax Partners. Before becoming active in business, Kestenbaum started his career in education, building an international training programme for promising young educators. He subsequently helped establish and build a large family commodity trading business, and then moved to public service, becoming Chief Executive of the Office of the Chief Rabbi, Professor Jonathan Sacks. In 1996 he was appointed Chief Executive of the United Jewish Israel Appeal (UJIA), one of the largest voluntary organisations in the UK.

Dr Gerry Lawless

Dr Gerry Lawless has been head of the chemistry department at the University of Sussex since 2004 and a faculty member for almost 20 years. Most recently, he was chair of the University's working party which formulated the structure of the new science curriculum provision proposed for implementation in 2006. During his research career he has published over 40 papers, two book chapters and has been successful in obtaining over £1.5 million in research funding. His area expertise is NMR spectroscopy, supercritical fluids, and synthetic organometallic chemistry. Previously, Lawless was a research fellow at Yale University and a visiting professor at North Western University. He is also governor of a local school.

Dr Peter Martin

Peter Martin is an academic and engineer in the department of engineering science, University of Oxford, and tutors at Christ Church College, Oxford. He has a first class Honours degree in engineering from Oxford, and a PhD from the University of Cambridge. Aside from his academic research and teaching activities, Martin has a keen interest in public engagement in both educational and engineering affairs, such as the EPSRC-funded 'IDEAs in the Pipeline' project. He has held a Royal Academy of Engineering grant to research health and safety in Ghanaian industry, and has worked as Researcher in Residence at the Purse School, Cambridge.

Ian Mellor

Ian Mellor is former head of Stockport Grammar School. A teacher of modern languages, he was also an A-level examiner in German literature. He retired in 2005.

Helen O'Brien

Helen O'Brien is an instrumentation engineer at the Space Magnetometer Laboratory at Imperial College London. She completed a Master of Engineering degree at Trinity College, Cambridge in 1998, and spent four years as a drilling services engineer for Schlumberger Oilfield services before joining the Space and Atmospheric Physics Group at Imperial College in 2003. O'Brien was involved in the design and build of the magnetic field experiments for the two Double Star Earth orbiting scientific satellites and is now involved in developing a new generation of smaller, lighter instruments for future space missions investigating the magnetic fields of the Earth and beyond.

David Perks

David Perks is head of physics at Graveney School, London. After completing his PGCE at Oxford he went straight into teaching, and now has 20 years' teaching experience in state schools. Perks campaigns for the teaching of science through separate academic disciplines, and writes regularly on education issues, with a focus on defending academic science education in schools.

Michael Reiss

Michael Reiss is professor of science education at the Institute of Education in London, and director of education at the Royal Society. As an academic and policy-maker, he tries to find ways to improve how science is taught in schools and elsewhere. Professor Reiss co-authored *Learning Science Outside the Classroom*, published by Routledge Falmer in July 2004.

Dr Michael Sargent

Dr Michael Sargent is at the National Institute for Medical Research, Mill Hill, London. His career in research evolved from microbiology, through molecular biology to developmental biology. He co-ordinates a variety of outreach activities mounted by the Institute, and is the author of *Biomedicine and the Human Condition: Challenges, Risks and Rewards*, published by Cambridge University Press in 2005. During the winter of 2006 he visited Ethiopia and India on a Winston Churchill Travelling Fellowship.

Simon Singh

Simon Singh is a science writer and broadcaster with a particular interest in science education. He has taught for short periods in the UK, India and South Africa, and he has lectured at over 100 school events in the three years. He helped to start two successful school science projects, including the Undergraduate Ambassadors Scheme (UAS), which currently helps to place hundreds of undergraduates in classrooms each year. One of UAS's goals is to encourage these students to consider a career in teaching.

Sir Richard Sykes

Sir Richard Sykes DSc FRS FMedSci became Rector of Imperial College London in January 2001. He was awarded a BSc in microbiology from Queen Elizabeth College, University of London, a PhD in microbial biochemistry from Bristol University, and a DSc from the University of London. He received a knighthood in the 1994 New Year's Honours list for services to the pharmaceutical industry. Before joining Imperial College, Sir Richard had a 30-year career in pharmaceutical research and industry with Glaxo, subsequently Glaxo Wellcome, where he was Chairman and Chief Executive, and then GlaxoSmithKline, which he left as Chairman in 2002. He serves on a number of scientific, higher education and government committees, and holds a number of honorary degrees and awards from institutions both in the UK and overseas.

Harriet Teare

Harriet Teare is just starting her second year as a chemistry DPhil at the University of Oxford, in the research group of Veronique Gouverneur. Her research involves Fluorine-18 labelling in Positron Emission Tomography. When not in the lab she can often be found kick-boxing or on the river.

Baroness Mary Warnock

Mary Warnock is a moral philosopher and author of numerous books on philosophy, including *The Intelligent Person's Guide to Ethics*. She is a Life Fellow of Girton College, Cambridge, and an Honorary Fellow of Hertford College, Lady Margaret Hall, and St Hugh's College, Oxford. In 1984 she produced the influential 'Warnock Report', having chaired the Committee on Human Fertilisation and Embryology. She has also chaired and served in several other committees of enquiry dealing with the education of handicapped children, animal experimentation, higher education, teaching quality and bioethics. In 1985 she was made a life peer as Baroness Warnock of Weeke.